What is
Cultural History?

PETER BURKE

polity

First published in 2004 by Polity Press Ltd.

Polity Press
65 Bridge Street
Cambridge CB2 1UR, UK

Polity Press
350 Main Street
Malden, MA 02148, USA

ISBN: 0-7456 3074-X
ISBN: 0-7456 3075-8 (pb)

A catalogue record for this book is available from the British Library and has been applied for from the Library of Congress.

Typeset in 10.5 on 12 pt Sabon
by SNP Best-set Typesetter Ltd., Hong Kong
Printed and bound in Great Britain by TJ International Ltd, Padstow, Cornwall

For further information on Polity, visit our website: www.polity.co.uk

Contents

Acknowledgements

I have been lecturing about, as well as in, cultural history for so many years that it is difficult to remember who made which helpful comment or asked which provoking question, but I do know that I have learned much from the conversation as well as from the writings of a number of the historians discussed in this book, including Keith Thomas in Oxford, Daniel Roche, Roger Chartier and Denis Crouzet in Paris, Natalie Davis and Robert Darnton in Princeton, and a circle of Dutch historians including Anton Blok, Jan Bremmer, Rudolf Dekker, Florike Egmond and Herman Roodenburg. On the history of memory in particular I have learned from listening to Aleida and Jan Assmann and Jay Winter. Discussions with Patrick Chabal while he was writing his book on the cultural approach to politics, *Culture Troubles*, helped me define my own ideas as well as informing me about a neighbouring discipline. I also profited from the comments made by anonymous readers on the original proposal as well as on the penultimate version of the book.

I owe a particular debt to my wife, another cultural historian, Maria Lúcia Pallares-Burke. I first met her when she invited me to lecture on 'the so-called new history' at the University of São Paulo. We have discussed cultural history many times, especially when she was editing her book of interviews, *The New History: Confessions and Conversations*. She also read this book in manuscript and as usual made some indispensable suggestions for improving it. This book is for her.

Introduction

Cultural history, once a Cinderella among the disciplines, neglected by its more successful sisters, was rediscovered in the 1970s, as the chronological list of publications at the end of the volume suggests. It has been enjoying a revival ever since, at least in the academic world – the history presented on television, at least in Britain, remains predominantly military, political and, to a lesser extent, social. For someone like myself, who has been practising the discipline for some forty years, this revival of interest is extremely gratifying, but it still requires an explanation.

The purpose of this book is precisely to explain not only the rediscovery but also what cultural history is, or better, what cultural historians do, paying attention to varieties, debates and conflicts but also to shared concerns and traditions. In so doing, it will try to combine two opposite but complementary approaches: an internal approach concerned with the solving of successive problems within the discipline and an approach from outside relating what historians do to the time in which they live.

The internal approach treats the current revival of cultural history as a reaction against earlier approaches to the past which left out something at once elusive and important. According to this view from inside, the cultural historian gets to parts of the past that other historians cannot reach. The emphasis on whole 'cultures' offers a remedy for the current fragmentation of the discipline into specialists on the history of population, diplomacy, women, ideas, business, warfare and so on.

The external approach or view from outside also has something to offer. In the first place, it connects the rise of cultural history to a wider 'cultural turn' in political science, geography, economics, psychology, anthropology and 'cultural studies'. There has been a shift in these disciplines, at least among a minority of scholars, from the assumption of unchanging rationality (the rational choice theory of voting or consumption, for instance), to an increasing interest in the values held by particular groups in particular places and particular periods.

One sign of the times is the conversion of the American political scientist Samuel P. Huntington to the idea that in the world today, cultural distinctions are more important than political or economic ones, so that since the end of the Cold War what we see is not so much an international conflict of interests as a 'clash of civilizations'. Another indicator of the intellectual climate is the international success of Cultural Studies. In Russia, in the 1990s, for instance, *Kul'turologija* (as it is called there), became a compulsory course in higher education, concerned in particular with the Russian identity and often taught by ex-professors of Marx-Leninism who have been converted from an economic interpretation of history to a cultural one.[1]

This cultural turn is itself part of the cultural history of the last generation. Outside the academic domain, it is linked to a shift in perception expressed in increasingly common phrases such as 'the culture of poverty', 'culture of fear', 'gun culture', 'teen culture' or 'corporate culture' (see p. 31) as well as in the so-called 'culture wars' in the USA and the debate over 'multiculturalism' in many countries. Many people today speak of 'culture' on everyday occasions on which twenty or thirty years ago they would have spoken of 'society'.

As the popularity of phrases like these suggest, it is increasingly difficult to say what does not count as 'culture'. The study of history is no exception to this general trend. What is cultural history? The question was asked in public more than a century ago, in 1897, by a pioneering German historian who was also something of a maverick, Karl Lamprecht. For better or for worse, it still awaits a definitive answer. Readers have recently been offered cultural histories of longevity, the penis, barbed wire and masturbation. The frontiers of the subject have certainly been extended, but it is becoming more and more difficult to say exactly what they enclose.

One solution to the problem of defining cultural history might be to switch attention from the objects to the methods of study. Here too, though, what we find is variety and controversy. Some cultural historians work intuitively, as Jacob Burckhardt said he did. A few attempt to make use of quantitative methods. Some of them describe their work in terms of a search for meaning, others focus on practices and representations. Some see their aim as essentially descriptive, others believe that cultural history, like political history, can and should be presented as a story.

The common ground of cultural historians might be described as a concern with the symbolic and its interpretation. Symbols, conscious or unconscious, can be found everywhere, from art to everyday life, but an approach to the past in terms of symbolism is just one approach among others. A cultural history of trousers, for instance, would differ from an economic history of the same subject, just as a cultural history of Parliament would differ from a political history of the same institution.

In this situation of confusion (according to those who disapprove) or dialogue (for those who find it exciting), the wisest course may well be to adapt Jean-Paul Sartre's epigram on humanity and declare that although cultural history has no essence, it does have a history of its own. The activities of reading and writing about the past are as much time-bound as other activities. Hence this book will comment from time to time on the cultural history of cultural history, treating it as an example of a cultural tradition in perpetual transformation, constantly adapted to new circumstances.

To be a little more precise, the work of individual cultural historians needs to be replaced in one of several different cultural traditions, generally defined on national lines. The importance of the German tradition, from the end of the eighteenth century onwards, will become apparent in the pages that follow, though the relative lack of important German contributions to this kind of history in the last fifty years is a problem for a future cultural historian to address. The Dutch tradition may be seen as an offshoot of the German, but one which has continued to flourish. In the English-speaking world there is a significant contrast between the North American tradition of interest in cultural history and the English tradition of resistance to it. In similar fashion, for a number of years, British anthropologists described themselves as 'social', while their American colleagues called themselves 'cultural'. In the case of cultural history, it is, above all, the North Americans – especially the descendants of German-speaking immigrants, from Peter Gay to Carl Schorske – who have taken up or taken over the German tradition, transforming it as they did so. The link between the American interest in culture and the tradition of immigration appears to be a close one. If this is the case, cultural history in Britain should have a great future.

The French tradition is distinctive, among other things for avoiding the term 'culture' – until quite recently, at any rate – and for focusing instead on *civilisation, mentalités collectives*, and *imaginaire social*. The historians associated with the journal *Annales* have made a remarkable series of contributions to this field over three or four generations; to the history of mentalities, sensibilities or 'collective representations' in the age of Marc Bloch and Lucien Febvre; to the history of material culture (*civilisation matérielle*) in the age of Fernand Braudel; and to the history of mentalities (once again) and the social imagination in the age of Jacques Le Goff, Emmanuel Le Roy Ladurie and Alain Corbin. The sustained creativity of a school of historians over three or four generations is so remarkable as to require a historical explanation. My own suggestion, for what it is worth, is that the leaders were charismatic enough to attract gifted followers, but also open enough to let them develop in their own way. This distinctive tradition was associated with what might be called a 'resistance' to the German style of cultural history (though Febvre's enthusiasm for Johan Huizinga deserves to be noted). This resistance seems to be breaking down, at the moment that the French historiographical tradition is becoming less distinctive.

As in the history of culture more generally, we shall see in the following pages that movements or trends are often brought to an abrupt end not because they have exhausted their potential, but because they are supplanted by competitors. These competitors, the 'children' we may call them, regularly exaggerate the difference between their own approach and that of their fathers and mothers, leaving it to the following generation to realize that their intellectual grandparents were, after all, capable of some insights.

As a cultural historian who has practised over the years a number of the different approaches discussed in the following pages, from the social history of high and popular culture and historical anthropology to the history of performance, I should like to say with Edith Piaf that '*je ne regrette rien*' and that I see all these approaches as continuing to yield insights.

The following chapters will deal in chronological order with some of the principal ways in which cultural history used to be written, is written today, and will be written, may be written or should be written in the future. In discussing concrete examples I have tried, so far as my partial knowledge of a fragmented field allows, to strike some sort of balance between different historical periods, different parts of the world, and the productions of different academic departments, including departments of art, architecture, geography, literature, music and science as well as plain 'history'.

The price of this decision has necessarily been to omit a good deal of exciting work in the early modern field, much of it by friends and colleagues of mine. Let me therefore make the point here, once and for all, that what follows is a survey of trends illustrated by examples, and not an attempt to list or discuss all the best work produced in the last generation.

Studies cited in the text use the titles of the English translations, where appropriate, but give the date of original publication. Where a place of publication is not given in a work cited in the notes, it is London. Information about technical terms and about individuals mentioned in the text will be found in the index.

1
The Great Tradition

Cultural history is not a new discovery or invention. It was already practised in Germany under that name (*Kulturgeschichte*) more than two hundred years ago. Before this time, there were separate histories of philosophy, painting, literature, chemistry, language and so on. From the 1780s onwards, we find histories of human culture or the culture of particular regions or nations.[1]

In the nineteenth century, the term 'Culture' or 'Kultur' was employed more and more often in Britain and in Germany (the French preferred to speak of *civilisation*). Thus the poet Matthew Arnold published his *Culture and Anarchy* in 1869, and the anthropologist Edward Tylor his *Primitive Culture* in 1871, while in Germany in the 1870s, a bitter conflict between Church and State became known as the 'struggle for culture' (*Kulturkampf*), or as we say today, 'culture wars'.[2]

In a brief chapter such as this there is only room to sketch the history of cultural history, taking a few of the main threads and showing how they were interwoven. The story may be divided into four phases: the 'classic' phase; the phase of the 'social history of art', which began in the 1930s; the discovery of the history of popular culture in the 1960s; and the 'new cultural history', which will be discussed in later chapters. However, it is worth bearing in mind that the divisions between these phases were not as clear at the time as people remember them after the event, and a number of similarities or continuities between older and newer styles of cultural history will be pointed out in the appropriate places.

Classic Cultural History

Portraits of an age

The period from about 1800 to 1950 was the age of what might be called 'classic' cultural history. Borrowing the phrase coined by the English critic F. R. Leavis to describe the novel, we might speak of a 'great tradition'. This tradition included classics such as the Swiss historian Jacob Burckhardt's *Civilization of the Renaissance in Italy*, first published in 1860, and the Dutch historian Johan Huizinga's *Autumn of the Middle Ages* (1919), two books that remain well worth reading. Implicit in both works is the idea of the historian as painting the 'portrait of an age', to quote the sub-title of a third classic, G. M. Young's *Victorian England* (1936).

This period might also be called the 'classic' period in the sense of the time when cultural historians concentrated on the history of the classics, a 'canon' of masterpieces of art, literature, philosophy, science and so on. Burckhardt and Huizinga were both amateur artists as well as art-lovers and they began their famous books in order to understand certain works by placing them in their historical context, the paintings of the van Eyck brothers in Huizinga's case and those of Raphael in that of Burckhardt.[3]

The difference between these scholars and the specialist historians of art or literature was that cultural historians concerned themselves in particular with the connections between the different arts. They discussed the connections in terms of the relation of these different arts to what was often called, following Hegel and other philosophers, the 'spirit of the age', or *Zeitgeist*.

Hence some German historians described themselves at this time as doing *Geistesgeschichte*, a term which is often translated as 'history of spirit' or 'history of mind' but may also be rendered as 'history of culture'. Its practitioners 'read' specific paintings, poems, etc. as evidence of the culture and the period in which they were produced. In so doing they widened the idea of hermeneutics, the art of interpretation. The term 'hermeneutics' originally referred to interpretations of texts, especially the Bible, but it expanded in the nineteenth century to include the interpretation of artefacts and actions.

It is surely no accident that the greatest cultural historians of the period, Jacob Burckhardt and Johan Huizinga, although they were professional academics, wrote their books primarily for a wider public. Nor is it an accident that cultural history developed in the German-speaking world before the unification of Germany, when the nation was a cultural community rather than a political one, or that cultural and political history came to be viewed as alternatives or even opposites. In Prussia, however, political history was dominant. Cultural history was dismissed by the followers of Leopold von Ranke as marginal or amateurish, since it was not based on official documents from archives and did not help in the task of state-building.[4]

In his scholarly work, Burckhardt ranged widely, from ancient Greece via the early Christian centuries and the Italian Renaissance to the world of the Flemish painter Peter Paul Rubens. He gave relatively little emphasis to the history of events, preferring to evoke a past culture and to stress what he called 'the recurrent, the constant and the typical' elements in it. He worked intuitively, steeping himself in the art and literature of the period he was studying and producing generalizations which he illustrated with examples, anecdotes and quotations, evoked in his vivid prose.

For example, in his most famous book Burckhardt described what he called the individualism, competitiveness, self-consciousness and modernity in the art, literature, philosophy and even in the politics of Renaissance Italy. In his posthumously published *Cultural History of Greece*, Burckhardt returned to this theme, noting the place of contest (*agon*) in ancient Greek life, in war, politics and music as well as in chariot-racing or the Olympic Games. Where the earlier book had emphasized the development of the individual, the later one stressed the tension between what the author calls 'unregenerate individualism' and the passion for fame on one side, and on the other the demand that the individual subordinate himself to his city. Huizinga also ranged widely, from ancient India to the West and from twelfth-century France to Dutch culture in the seventeenth century and the USA in his own day. He was at once a critic of Burckhardt's interpretation of the Renaissance – which he thought distinguished it too sharply from the Middle Ages – and a follower of his method. In an essay that appeared in 1915, Huizinga discussed a variety of ideals of life, visions of the golden age, for instance, the cult of chivalry or the classical ideal that appealed so strongly to European elites between the Renaissance and the French Revolution.

In another essay, published in 1929, Huizinga declared that the principal aim of the cultural historian is to portray patterns of culture, in other words to describe the characteristic thoughts and feelings of an age and their expressions or embodiments in works of literature and art. The historian, he suggested, discovers these patterns of culture by studying 'themes', 'symbols', 'sentiments' and 'forms'. Forms, in other words cultural rules, were important for Huizinga in his life as in his work, and he found what he called 'the absence of a sense of form' an obstacle to his enjoyment of American literature.[5]

Huizinga's *Autumn of the Middle Ages* puts into practice the recommendations that he made in his programmatic essays. It is concerned with ideals of life such as chivalry. It deals with themes such as the sense of decline, with the place of symbolism in late medieval art and thought and with sentiments such as the fear of death. The book gives a central place to forms or standards of behaviour. According to Huizinga, 'the passionate and violent mind of the time' needed a framework of formality. Like piety, love and war were ritualized, aestheticized and subjected to rules. In this period, 'Every event, every action, was still embodied in expressive and solemn forms, which raised them to the dignity of a ritual.'

One might say that Huizinga's approach to cultural history was essentially a morphological one. He was concerned with the style of a whole culture as well as the style of individual paintings and poems.

This programme for cultural history was not as abstract as it may sound when summarized briefly. 'What sort of idea can we form of an age', Huizinga once wrote, 'if we see no people in it? If we may only give generalized accounts we do but make a desert and call it history.' In fact his *Middle Ages* is swarming with individuals, from the picaresque poet François Villon to the mystic Heinrich Suso, from the popular preacher Olivier Maillard to the courtly chronicler Georges Chastellain. The prose is sensuous, attentive to sounds such as bells and drums as well as to visual images. The book is a literary masterpiece in a fin de siècle style as well as a historical classic.

From sociology to art history

Some of the greatest contributions to cultural history in this period, especially in Germany, came from scholars who worked outside history departments. The sociologist Max Weber published a famous work, *The Protestant Ethic and the Spirit of Capitalism* (1904) which analysed the cultural roots of what he called 'the economic system prevailing in Western Europe and America'. Weber's essay might equally well have been entitled 'Capitalism and the Culture of Protestantism' or 'Protestantism and the Culture of Capitalism'.

The point of the essay was essentially to offer a cultural explanation of economic change, stressing the role of the Protestant ethos or value-system, especially the idea of a 'calling', for the accumulation of capital and the rise of commerce and industry on a grand scale. In another study, Weber argued that the ethos of Confucianism, like that of Catholicism, was hostile to capitalism (he would have been surprised to learn of the rise of the 'tiger' economies).

In the next generation, another German sociologist, Norbert Elias, a follower of Weber in certain respects, produced a study, *The Civilizing Process* (1939), which is essentially a cultural history. He also drew on Freud's *Civilization and its Discontents* (1930), which argued that culture requires sacrifices from the individual, in the sphere of sex and in the sphere of aggression.

Building on the research of Huizinga on 'the passionate and violent mind of the time', Elias focused on the history of table manners in order to show the gradual development at the courts of Western Europe of self-control or control over the emotions, linking what he called the 'social pressures toward self-control' between the fifteenth and the eighteenth centuries to the centralization of government and the taming or domestication of a warrior nobility.

Elias claimed to be writing about 'civilization' rather than culture, 'the surface of human existence' rather than its depths, the history of the fork and the handkerchief rather than that of the human spirit. All the same, he made a major contribution to the study of what might well be described today as 'the culture of self-control'.

One of the most original and ultimately one of the most influential figures in cultural history in the German style did not follow an academic career at all. Aby Warburg was a man of private means, a banker's son who renounced his inheritance in favour of a younger brother in return for an allowance large enough for him to buy all the books he needed – and he turned out to need many books, since his wide interests included philosophy, psychology and anthropology as well as the cultural history of the West from ancient Greece to the seventeenth century. His great aim was to contribute to a general 'science of culture' (*Kulturwissenschaft*), avoiding what he called the 'frontier police' on the borders between scholarly disciplines.

Warburg was a great admirer of Burckhardt and his 'unerring intuitive generalizations', but his own work was both richer and more fragmentary. Convinced that 'God is in the detail', he preferred writing essays on particular aspects of Renaissance Italy to what he called 'the great objective of a synthesis of cultural history'.[6] Warburg was particularly concerned with the classical tradition and its transformations over the long term. In studying this tradition he focused on cultural or perceptual schemata or formulae, gestures that express particular emotions, for instance, or the way in which poets and painters represented the wind in a girl's hair.

The idea of the schema has proved enormously stimulating for cultural historians and others. It has been argued by psychologists that it is impossible to perceive or remember anything without schemata. Some philosophers agree. Karl Popper argued that it was impossible to observe nature properly without having a hypothesis to test, a principle of selection that would allow the observer to see pattern rather than confusion. In similar fashion, Hans-Georg Gadamer claimed that the interpretation of texts depended on what he called *Vorurteil*, in other words 'prejudice' or, more exactly, 'prejudgement'.

Students of literature have moved in a similar direction. In his *European Literature and the Latin Middle Ages* (1948), a book dedicated to the memory of Warburg, Ernst-Robert Curtius demonstrated the enduring importance of rhetorical topoi or commonplaces such as the ideal landscape, the world turned upside-down or the metaphor of the 'book of nature'. William Tindall's study of John Bunyan (discussed in chapter 5, p. 89) is another example of a study of texts that concentrates on schemata.

However, it is surely in the work of Ernst Gombrich that the idea of the cultural schema was developed most fully. Gombrich, who wrote Warburg's intellectual biography, also drew on experimental psychology and the philosophy of Popper. In his *Art and Illusion* (1960), Gombrich's central theme was the relation between what he variously calls 'truth and the stereotype', 'formula and experience' or 'schema and correction'. Thus he described the rise of naturalism in ancient Greek art as 'the gradual accumulation of corrections due to the observation of reality'.

Cultural innovations are often the work of small groups rather than individuals. The importance of Aby Warburg does not reside in his essays alone, brilliant as they are, but also in his central position in a group of scholars who used to meet in his library in Hamburg, the nucleus of the later Warburg Institute. These scholars, united by an interest in the history of symbols as well as in the classical tradition, included the philosopher Ernst Cassirer, author of *The Philosophy of Symbolic Forms* (1923–9), and the art historians Fritz Saxl, Edgar Wind and Erwin Panofsky.

Panofsky, for instance, wrote a classic essay on the interpretation of images, a visual hermeneutics that distinguished 'iconography' (the interpretation of the subject matter of a *Last Supper*, for instance) from a broader 'iconology', which discovers the world-view of a culture or social group 'condensed into one work'.[7] Another famous example of the iconological approach, from a later period in Panofsky's career, is his provocative lecture 'Gothic Architecture and Scholasticism' (1951). This lecture is exemplary in its explicit and self-conscious focus on possible connections between different cultural domains.

Panofsky began from the observation that Gothic architecture and the scholastic philosophy associated with Thomas Aquinas arose at the same time, the twelfth and thirteenth centuries, and in the same place, in or near Paris. The two movements developed in parallel. However, the point of the lecture was not simply to trace a parallel between architecture and philosophy. Panofsky also claimed that there was a connection between the two movements.

This connection he discussed not in terms of the 'spirit of the age' but, more precisely, in terms of the spread from philosophy to architecture of what he calls a 'mental habit', a cluster of assumptions about the need for transparent organization and the reconciliation of contradictions. Aware that he might be criticized – as indeed he was – for speculation, Panofsky pounced on a 'scrap of evidence', a remark recorded in an album of sketches about two architects conducting a 'disputation' and so showing 'that at least some of the French thirteenth-century architects did think and act in strictly Scholastic terms'.

The great diaspora

By the time that his lecture on Gothic architecture and scholasticism was delivered, Panofsky had been living in the USA for a number of years. When Hitler came to power in 1933, Aby Warburg was dead, but the other scholars associated with his Institute took refuge abroad. The Institute itself, under threat because its founder was Jewish, was transferred – or, one might say, 'translated' – to London, together with Saxl and Wind, while Cassirer, like Panofsky – and Ernst Kantorowicz, another scholar concerned with the history of symbols – ended up in the United States. The consequences of this move for the two host countries, for cultural history in general and for art history in particular have been very great. The episode is an important part of the story of the great diaspora of Central Europeans, most of them Jewish, in the 1930s, including scientists, writers and musicians as well as scholars.[8] It also illustrates a favourite Warburgian theme, that of the transmission and transformation of cultural traditions.

In the United States in the earlier twentieth century, the keyword was 'civilization' rather than 'culture', as in Charles and Mary Beard's *The Rise of American Civilization* (1927). 'Civilization' courses were beginning at this time, thanks to the movement known as 'the New History' in which the Beards and other radical historians were involved. At Columbia College for instance, there was a required freshman course in the 1920s on Contemporary Civilization. By the middle of the century, many American universities were requiring courses in 'Western Civ', more or less a brief history of the western world from the ancient Greeks to the present, 'from Plato to NATO'.[9]

At the research level, on the other hand, a stronger or at any rate a more visible American tradition than that of cultural history was the 'history of ideas' exemplified by Perry Miller's *The New England Mind* (1939) and by the circle of Arthur Lovejoy at Johns Hopkins University, centred on the *Journal of the History of Ideas*, founded in 1940 as an interdisciplinary project linking philosophy, literature and history.

In Britain in the 1930s, some intellectual and cultural history was being written, generally outside history departments. Among the most important contributions to this tradition were Basil Willey's *The Seventeenth-Century Background* (1934), 'studies in the thought of the age', written by a professor of English and presented as 'background' to literature; E. M. W. Tillyard's *The Elizabethan World Picture* (1943), another contribution from the Cambridge Faculty of English; and G. M. Young's *Victorian England* (1936), the work of a gifted amateur.

The main exceptions to the emphasis on ideas were Christopher Dawson's *The Making of Europe* (1932), written at a time when the author was 'Lecturer in the History of Culture' at the University of Exeter; Arnold Toynbee's multivolume *Study of History* (1934–61), focusing on twenty-one separate 'civilizations', and written by the Director of the Royal Institute of International Affairs; and the biochemist Joseph Needham's monumental study, *Science and Civilization in China*, planned in the 1930s, although the first volume did not appear until 1954. It is worthy of remark that one of the rare explicit contributions to cultural history published in Britain in the middle of the twentieth century should have been written by a scientist.

As in the United States, the great diaspora was important in the rise of cultural history in Britain, as for art history, sociology and certain styles of philosophy. As an example of the effects of the encounter one might cite that very English scholar Frances Yates, originally a Shakespearean specialist. A meeting at a dinner party in the late 1930s led to her entry into the Warburg circle, at a time when, as she put it later, 'inspiring scholars and an inspiring library were recently arrived from Germany'. Yates was 'initiated into the Warburgian technique of using visual evidence as historical evidence'. Her interest in occult studies – Neoplatonism, magic, *Kabbalah* – was another result of that encounter.[10]

The diaspora also included a group of Marxists concerned with the relation between culture and society.

Culture and Society

In the USA, as in Britain, a certain interest in the relation between culture and society was already apparent before the arrival of the great diaspora. An early example of a social history of culture is that of the Beards, a couple with an important place in the history of American radicalism. As a student at Oxford, Charles Beard helped found Ruskin Hall to give the working class access to higher education (appropriately enough, this institution, by that time known as Ruskin College, was the cradle of the History Workshop movement). Returning to the USA, Beard became well known for his controversial study, *An Economic Interpretation of the Constitution of the United States* (1913).

Together with his wife Mary Ritter Beard, a leading suffragette and a campaigner for women's studies, Charles Beard wrote *The Rise of American Civilization* (1927), a study that offered an economic and social interpretation of cultural change. The final chapter on 'the Machine Age', for instance, discussed the role of the automobile in the spread of urban values and 'stereotyped mental excitements', the patronage of the arts by millionaires, the practical and popular emphasis of American science and the rise of jazz.

All the same, the arrival of a group of émigré scholars from Central Europe made both British and American scholars more sharply aware of the relation between culture and society. In the British case, a crucial role was played by three Hungarians, the sociologist Karl Mannheim, his friend Arnold Hauser and the art historian Frederick Antal.[11] All three were former members of a discussion group or 'Sunday circle' that centred on the critic Georg Lukács and met during the First World War. All three emigrated to England in the 1930s. Mannheim moved from a chair in Frankfurt to a lectureship at the London School of Economics and Antal from a chair in Central Europe to a lectureship at the Courtauld Institute, while Hauser became a freelance writer.

Mannheim, an admirer of Marx rather than a strict Marxist, had a particular interest in the sociology of knowledge, which he approached in a historical manner, for example by studying the mentality of German conservatives. While living in Germany he had some intellectual influence on two figures already mentioned in this chapter, Norbert Elias and Erwin Panofsky, although Panofsky abandoned the social approach.

In his books and essays Antal approached culture as an expression or even a 'reflection' of society. He viewed the art of Renaissance Florence as the reflection of the world-view of the bourgeoisie and he found William Hogarth interesting because 'his art reveals . . . the views and tastes of a broad cross-section of society'.[12] Antal's British disciples included Francis Klingender, author of *Art and the Industrial Revolution* (1947), Anthony Blunt, who was famous as an art historian long before he became notorious as a spy, and John Berger, who also approaches art from a social perspective.

As for Arnold Hauser, a more conventional Marxist, he was most important for spreading knowledge of the group's approach by writing a *Social History of Art* (1951), which linked culture closely to economic and social conflict and change, discussing, for instance, 'the class struggles in Italy at the end of the Middle Ages', 'Romanticism as a middle-class movement' and the relation between 'the film age' and 'the crisis of capitalism'.

Klingender, Blunt and Berger should be viewed not as simple cases of Hungarian influence but rather of 'reception' or cultural encounters. On one side, there was the problem of cultural resistance, leading Mannheim to complain about the difficulty of transplanting or 'translating' sociology to Britain. On the other side, some intellectual circles were already prepared for the reception of Mannheim's ideas. A small group of British Marxist intellectuals were active in the 1930s and 1940s both inside and outside academia. Roy Pascal, Professor of German at Birmingham from 1939 to 1969, wrote on the social history of literature. The classicist George Thomson's famous study of drama and society, *Aeschylus and Athens* (1941) was clearly inspired by Marx. Joseph Needham used a Marxist framework for his *Science and Civilization in China*.

F. R. Leavis, the author of *The Great Tradition* (1948), was also keenly interested in the relation between culture and its environment. His emphasis on the dependence of literature on 'a social culture and an art of living' owed less to Marx than to nostalgia for the traditional 'organic community'. However, it was not difficult to combine a 'Leavisite' with a Marxist approach, as Raymond Williams did in *The Long Revolution* (1961), a book which discussed the social history of drama as well as coining the famous phrase 'structures of feeling'.

The Discovery of the People

The idea of 'popular culture' or *Volkskultur* originated in the same place and time as 'cultural history': in Germany in the late eighteenth century. Folksongs, folktales, dances, rituals, arts and crafts were discovered by middle-class intellectuals at this time.[13] However, the history of this popular culture was left to antiquarians, folklorists and anthropologists. It was only in the 1960s that a group of academic historians turned to the study of popular culture.

An early example, published in 1959, was *The Jazz Scene*, written by 'Francis Newton', one of the pseudonyms of Eric Hobsbawm. As one might have expected from a distinguished economic and social historian, the author discussed not only the music but also the public who listened to it, not to mention jazz as business and as a form of social and political protest. He concluded that jazz exemplified the situation 'when a folk-music does not go under, but maintains itself in the environment of modern urban and industrial civilization'. Full of perceptive observations on the history of popular culture, this book never made the impact on the academic world that it deserved.

The most influential of the studies made in the 1960s was Edward Thompson's *Making of the English Working Class* (1963). In this book, Thompson did not confine himself to analysing the role in class formation played by economic and political changes, but examined the place of popular culture in this process. His book included vivid descriptions of the initiation rituals of artisans, the place of fairs in 'the cultural life of the poor', the symbolism of food and the iconography of riots, from banners or loaves of bread on sticks to the effigies of hate-figures hanged in the streets. Dialect poetry was analysed in order to reach what Thompson described – in the phrase of Raymond Williams – as 'a working-class structure of feeling'. Methodism received the lion's share of attention, from the style of lay preaching to the imagery of hymns, with special emphasis on the displacement of 'emotional and spiritual energies' which were 'confiscated for the service of the Church'.

Thompson's influence on younger historians has been very great. It is obvious in the History Workshop movement, founded in the 1960s under the leadership of Raphael Samuel. Samuel, who taught at Ruskin College Oxford, a centre for mature working-class students, organized many conferences, which he preferred to call 'workshops', founded a journal, *History Workshop*, and through his innumerable articles and seminar papers inspired many people to write history (including cultural history) 'from below'. The charismatic Thompson has also inspired historians of popular culture from Germany to India (see p. 104).

Why did a concern with the history of popular culture emerge when it did? There are, as usual, two principal explanations, the 'internal' and the 'external'. Insiders see themselves as responding to the deficiencies of earlier approaches, notably to cultural history with ordinary people left out and to political and economic history with the culture left out. They also tend to see themselves and their network as the sole innovators, and rarely notice parallel trends in other parts of the discipline, let alone in other disciplines or in the world outside the academy.

Outsiders tend to see a larger picture, to note that in Britain, for instance, the rise of the history of popular culture in the 1960s coincided with the rise of 'cultural studies', following the model of the Centre for Contemporary Cultural Studies at the University of Birmingham directed by Stuart Hall. The international success of the movement for cultural studies suggests that it responded to a demand, to a critique of the emphasis on a traditional high culture in schools and universities and also to the need to understand the changing world of commodities, advertising and television.

Like the great tradition and the Marxist approach, the history of popular culture posed problems that became more and more apparent over the years. These problems will be discussed in the following chapter.

2
Problems of Cultural History

As in the case of so many human activities, every solution
to the problem of writing cultural history sooner or later
generates problems of its own. If we were to stop reading
Burckhardt, the loss would be ours. All the same, we would
be ill-advised to imitate his work closely, not only because his
bow is a difficult one to bend and demands a degree of sensibility that most of us lack. Viewed from a distance of more
than a century, some weaknesses in his books, as in those of
Huizinga and other classics, have become apparent. The
sources, the methods and the assumptions of these studies all
need to be questioned.

The Classics Revisited

Take, for example, the way in which the evidence is handled
in the classics of cultural history. Huizinga's *Autumn of the
Middle Ages* in particular used a few literary sources again
and again. Using other writers might have produced a rather
different picture of the age. The temptation to which the cultural historian must not succumb is that of treating the texts
and images of a certain period as mirrors, unproblematic
reflections of their times.

In his book on Greece, Burckhardt argued for the relative reliability of the conclusions drawn by cultural historians. The political history of ancient Greece, he suggested, was full of uncertainties because the Greeks exaggerated or even lied. 'Cultural history by contrast possesses a primary degree of certainty, as it consists for the most part of material conveyed in an unintentional, disinterested or even involuntary way by sources and monuments.'[1]

So far as relative reliability is concerned, Burckhardt surely had a point. His argument about 'involuntary' testimony is also convincing: witnesses from the past can tell us things that they did not know they knew. All the same, it would be unwise to assume that novels, say, or paintings are always disinterested, free from passion or propaganda. Like their colleagues in political or economic history, cultural historians need to practise source criticism, to ask why a given text or image came into existence, whether for example its purpose was to persuade viewers or readers to take some course of action.

So far as method is concerned, Burckhardt and Huizinga have often been criticized as impressionistic and even anecdotal. It is well known that what we notice or remember is what interests us personally or fits in with what we already believe, but historians have not always reflected on the moral of this observation. 'Thirty years ago', the economic historian John Clapham once confessed, 'I read and marked Arthur Young's *Travels in France* and taught from the marked passages. Five years ago I went through it again to find that whenever Young spoke of a wretched Frenchman I had marked him, but that many of his references to happy or prosperous Frenchmen remained unmarked.' It may be suspected that Huizinga did something of the same kind when he was illustrating his claim that 'No other epoch laid so much stress as the expiring Middle Ages on the thought of death'.

Is cultural history condemned to be impressionistic? If not, what is the alternative? One possibility is what the French call 'serial history', in other words the analysis of a chronological series of documents. In the 1960s, some French historians were already working in this way on the spread of literacy and the 'history of the book'. For example, they compared the numbers of books published on different subjects in different decades in eighteenth-century France.[2] The serial approach to texts is appropriate in many domains of cultural history and has indeed been employed to analyse wills, charters, political pamphlets and so on. Images too have been analysed in this way, for example votive images from a particular region – Provence, for instance – that reveal changes in religious or social attitudes over the centuries.[3]

The problem raised by Clapham about subjective readings of texts is rather more difficult to resolve. However, there is a possible alternative to reading in this way. The alternative used to be known as 'content analysis', a method which was used in schools of journalism in the USA in the early twentieth century before it was adopted during the Second World War as a means for the Allies to obtain reliable information from German news bulletins. The procedure is to choose a text or corpus of texts, count the frequency of references to a given theme or themes, and analyse 'covariance', in other words the association of some themes with others.

For example, one might analyse the historical writings of Tacitus in this way, noting the remarkable frequency of words for 'fear' (*metus*, *pavor*) and treating them as evidence for the author's conscious or unconscious insecurity.[4] In the 1970s, a group describing itself as a 'Laboratory of Lexicometry', based at Saint-Cloud and working on the French Revolution, listed the most common themes in texts by Rousseau, Robespierre and others, noting, for example, that the most common noun in Rousseau's Social Contract was *loi* (law), while in texts by Robespierre it was *peuple* (people), and that Robespierre tended to associate the term *peuple* with *droits* (rights) and *souveraineté* (sovereignty).[5]

Content analysis of this kind has some awkward questions to answer. The work of the Saint-Cloud group was purely descriptive, and it may be argued that it is not worth investing this effort without a hypothesis to test. In any case, the move from words to themes is a difficult one. The same word carries different meanings in different contexts, and themes may be modified by association with one another. A quantitative approach is too mechanical, too insensitive to variation, to be illuminating by itself.

Used in combination with traditional literary methods of close reading, though, content analysis does at least correct the kind of bias described by Clapham. A similar point might be made about 'discourse analysis', the linguistic analysis of texts longer than a single sentence, an approach with more than a little in common with the content analysis it has supplanted, though it pays more attention to everyday speech, to verbal schemata, to literary genres and to forms of narrative.[6]

Another kind of problem, that of assumptions, is emphasized in Ernst Gombrich's lecture 'In Search of Cultural History', which is a critique of Burckhardt, Huizinga and also of Marxists, notably Hauser, for building their cultural history on 'Hegelian foundations', in other words the idea of the *Zeitgeist*, so popular in the German-speaking world at the turn of the eighteenth and nineteenth centuries.[7] In what follows, however, I shall contrast the Burckhardtian and the Marxist approaches to culture, discussing first the Marxist critique of the classics, and then the problems raised by a Marxist history of culture.

Marxist Debates

The main Marxist critique of the classic approach to culture is that it is 'in the air', lacking contact with any economic or social base. Burckhardt had little to say, as he later admitted, about the economic foundations of the Italian Renaissance, while Huizinga virtually ignored the Black Death in his account of the sense of mortality in the later Middle Ages. Again, Panofsky's essay had little to say about the contacts between the two social groups responsible for the achievements of Gothic architecture and scholasticism, the master masons and the masters of arts.

A second Marxist critique of the classic cultural historians is to accuse them of overestimating cultural homogeneity and of ignoring cultural conflicts. A memorably trenchant expression of this critique can be found in an essay by Edward Thompson in which he calls culture 'a clumpish term', lumping things together, hiding distinctions, and tending to 'nudge us towards over-consensual and holistic notions'.[8] Distinctions need to be drawn between the cultures of social classes, the cultures of men and women, and the cultures of different generations living in the same society.

Another useful distinction is the one between what might be called 'time-zones'. As the German Marxist Ernst Bloch suggested in the 1930s, 'Not all people exist in the same Now. They do so only externally, through the fact that they can be seen today.' In fact, 'they carry an earlier element with them; this interferes'.[9] Bloch was thinking of the German peasants of the 1930s, or the impoverished middle class of his time, who were living in the past. However, the 'contemporaneity of the non-contemporary', as he put it, is a much more general historical phenomenon that undermines the old assumption of the cultural unity of an age.

This point might be illustrated from the history of cultural history itself, since the classical approach, the social history of culture and the history of popular culture have long co-existed.

Problems of Marxist history

The Marxist approach itself raises awkward problems. To be a Marxist historian of culture is to live a paradox if not a contradiction. Why should Marxists concern themselves with what Marx dismissed as a mere 'superstructure'?

Retrospectively, Edward Thompson's famous study, *The Making of the English Working Class* (1963), appears as a milestone in the history of British cultural history. When it was published, on the other hand, Thompson's book was criticized by some fellow-Marxists for what they called its 'culturalism', in other words for placing its emphasis on experience and ideas rather than on hard economic social and political realities. The author's response was to criticize his critics for their 'economism'.

This tension between culturalism and economism was a creative one, at least on occasion. It encouraged a critique from within of the central Marxist concepts of an economic and social foundation or 'base' and a cultural 'superstructure'. Raymond Williams, for example, described the formula of base and superstructure as a 'rigid' one, preferring to study what he called 'relations between elements in a whole way of life'. Williams was attracted by the idea of 'cultural hegemony', that is, the suggestion – made by the Italian Marxist Antonio Gramsci, among others – that the ruling classes rule not only directly, through force and the threat of force, but because their ideas have come to be accepted by the 'subordinate classes' (*classi subalterni*).[10]

For Thompson too, the idea of cultural hegemony offered a better formulation of the relation between culture and society than did 'superstructure'. As he put it in *Whigs and Hunters* (1975), with his characteristic rhetoric:

> The hegemony of the eighteenth-century gentry and aristocracy was expressed, above all, not in military force, not in the mystifications of priesthood and the press, not even in economic coercion, but in the rituals of the study of the Justices of the Peace, in the quarter-sessions, in the pomp of Assizes and in the theatre of Tyburn.

Problems remain. For one thing, a Marxism that dispenses with the complementary notions of base and superstructure is in danger of losing its distinctive qualities. For another, Thompson's critique of 'holistic notions' seems to render cultural history impossible, or at any rate to reduce it to fragments. Different as the two scholars were, Thompson seems to point in the same direction as Gombrich when he was rejecting the 'Hegelian foundations' of the syntheses of Burckhardt and Huizinga. These criticisms raise a fundamental question: is it possible to study cultures as wholes without making false assumptions about cultural homogeneity?

Two main answers to this question have been proposed. One is to study cultural traditions, and the other is to treat learned and popular culture as 'sub-cultures', partially but not wholly separate or autonomous.

The Paradoxes of Tradition

The idea of culture implies the idea of tradition, of certain kinds of knowledge and skills handed down from one generation to the next. Since multiple traditions can easily co-exist in the same society – lay and clerical, male and female, that of the pen and that of the sword, and so on – to work with the idea of tradition liberates cultural historians from the assumption of the unity or homogeneity of an 'age' – the Middle Ages, the age of Enlightenment, or whatever. Among the historians who were mentioned in the previous chapter, Aby Warburg and Ernst-Robert Curtius were particularly concerned with tradition, in their cases the fate of the classical tradition in the post-classical world.

The idea of tradition seems virtually self-evident, yet this traditional notion of tradition, as we may call it, needs to be seen as problematic. The two main problems might be described as the twin paradoxes of tradition.

In the first place, apparent innovation may mask the persistence of tradition. The persistence of religious attitudes in a secularized form has been noted in many cultures, Catholic, Protestant, Jewish, Hindu and Muslim. The survival of certain Puritan attitudes and values in the United States today is an obvious example – the sense of the importance of the individual, for instance, or the need for achievement, or the concern with self-scrutiny. Historians of missions used to concentrate on the 'conversion' of individuals, groups and peoples from one religion to another. Today, aware of the persistence of tradition, they place more emphasis on the conscious or unconscious mixture or synthesis of the beliefs and values of the two religions involved.

Conversely, the outward signs of tradition may mask innovation. Marx's quip that he was not a Marxist is well known. It seems to refer to a recurrent problem that may be described as the problem of founders and followers. The message of a successful founder of a movement, philosophy or religion is rarely simple. It appeals to many people because it has many aspects. Some followers emphasize one aspect, others another, according to their own interests or the situation in which they find themselves. Even more fundamental is the problem of the 'inner conflict of traditions', the inevitable conflict between universal rules and specific, ever-changing situations.[11]

In other words, what is handed down changes – indeed, has to change – in the course of transmission to a new generation. The great weakness of the study of European literature by Curtius is the author's reluctance to recognize this fact and to treat the commonplaces he studied as constants. By contrast, Warburg was acutely aware of the modifications made to the classical tradition over the centuries. Today, cultural historians are even more interested in the question of 'reception', as we shall see in chapter 5.

Popular Culture in Question

To distinguish between learned culture and popular culture within a given society is another obvious alternative to the assumption of cultural homogeneity. However, like the concept of *Zeitgeist* and the idea of superstructure, the notion of 'popular culture' has itself become a matter for debate, a debate to which theorists such as Michel de Certeau and Stuart Hall, as well as historians such as Roger Chartier and Jacques Revel, have made valuable contributions.[12]

To begin with, there is the difficulty of defining the subject. Who are 'the people'? Everyone, or just the non-elite? If the latter, we are employing a residual category, and as usual in the case of residual categories, we run the danger of assuming the homogeneity of the excluded. It might be better to follow the example of a number of recent historians and theorists and to think of popular cultures in the plural, urban and rural, male and female, old and young and so on.

However, this solution generates a new problem. Is there, for example, an autonomous female culture, distinct from that of men in the same society? To say 'no' is to deny palpable difference, but to say 'yes' may well exaggerate that difference. It might be more illuminating to think in terms of more or less autonomous or bounded female cultures or 'subcultures', which are more autonomous whenever women are more sharply segregated from men; in nunneries for instance, in the traditional Mediterranean world, or in the culture of Islam.

In the case of ancient Greece, a classicist inspired by cultural anthropology, John Winkler, has shown that although the surviving sources are almost entirely the work of men, they may be read against the grain to reveal distinctively female views of sex and other matters. He treats Sappho's lyrics and the female festival of the Adonia as particularly valuable evidence of 'a different consciousness on the part of Greek women concerning the meanings of sex and gender from those enunciated by their husbands and fathers'.[13]

Another problem for historians of popular culture is whether they should include or exclude elites, at least in certain periods. What makes exclusion problematic is the fact that people with high status, great wealth or a substantial amount of power are not necessarily different in their culture from ordinary people. In seventeenth-century France, for instance, the readers of chap-books – cheap booklets traditionally described as examples of popular culture – included noblewomen and even a duchess. This is hardly surprising, since educational opportunities for females were severely limited at this time.

Hence, Roger Chartier has argued that it is virtually impossible to label either objects or cultural practices as 'popular'. Focusing on social groups rather than objects or practices, it may be argued that the elites of Western Europe in early modern times were 'bicultural', participating in what historians call 'popular culture' as well as in a learned culture from which ordinary people were excluded. It was only after the middle of the seventeenth century that the elites generally withdrew from participation in popular culture.[14]

Scholars have often pointed to the many interactions between learned and popular culture as a reason for abandoning the two adjectives altogether. The problem is that without these adjectives, the interactions between the learned and the popular become impossible to describe. The best policy, perhaps, is to employ the two terms without making the binary opposition too rigid, and to place both learned and popular in a wider framework. The French historian Georges Duby, for example, did this in a path-breaking article about the diffusion of cultural models in feudal society, examining the upward and downward movement of objects and practices without dividing the culture into two.[15]

What is Culture?

The term 'culture' is even more problematic than the term 'popular'. As Burckhardt remarked in 1882, cultural history is 'a vague concept'. It used to refer to 'high' culture. It was extended 'downwards', to continue the metaphor, to include 'low' or popular culture. More recently, it has expanded sideways as well. The term culture used to refer to the arts and sciences. Then it was used to describe the popular equivalents to the arts and sciences – folk music, folk medicine and so on. In the last generation, the word has come to refer to a wide range of artefacts (images, tools, houses and so on) and practices (conversation, reading, playing games).

This new usage is not, strictly speaking, new at all. In 1948, in his *Notes Towards the Definition of Culture*, T. S. Eliot, an American observing England with an anthropological eye, had described its culture as including, among other elements, 'Derby Day . . . the dart board . . . boiled cabbage cut into sections, beetroot in vinegar, nineteenth-century Gothic churches and the music of Elgar'. The anthropologist Bronisław Malinowski was already defining culture in a broad way, in the article on the subject that he contributed to the *Encyclopaedia of the Social Sciences* in 1931, as comprising 'inherited artefacts, goods, technical processes, ideas, habits and values'.

Indeed, in 1871, in his *Primitive Culture*, another anthropologist, Edward Tylor, had offered a similar definition of culture 'taken in its wide ethnographic sense', as 'that complex whole which includes knowledge, belief, art, morals, law, custom and any other capabilities and habits acquired by man as a member of society'. The anthropological concern with the everyday, and with societies in which there was relatively little division of labour, encouraged the employment of the term 'culture' in a wide sense.

It is this anthropological notion that cultural historians – and other members of their culture – have made their own in the last generation, the age of 'historical anthropology' and 'the new cultural history'. These twin movements are the subject of the following chapters.

3
The Moment of Historical Anthropology

One of the most distinctive features of the practice of cultural history, from the 1960s to the 1990s, has been the turn to anthropology. The turn was not confined to cultural history: some economic historians, for instance, studied economic anthropology. But even in this case the principal lesson they learned was a cultural one, about the importance of values in explaining the production, accumulation and consumption of wealth.

Many historians learned to use the term 'culture' in the broad sense discussed at the end of the last chapter. A few of them, especially in France, the USA and Britain, frequented anthropology seminars, borrowed concepts and worked out an approach that became known as 'historical anthropology', though 'anthropological history' might have been more appropriate. One of the most significant changes that followed this long moment of encounter between history and anthropology – an encounter that has not yet come to an end, although it is probably less close than it used to be – was the use of the term 'culture' in the plural and in an increasingly broad sense.

The Expansion of Culture

An interest in culture, cultural history and in 'cultural studies' became increasingly visible in the 1980s and 1990s. In different disciplines, though, this cultural turn has had different effects and even, perhaps, different meanings.

In the case of cultural psychology, for instance, it signifies a shift away from the idea that human beings have identical drives, and a rapprochement with sociology and anthropology. In cultural geography, the challenge is to avoid returning to the traditional idea of 'culture areas' that passes over social differences and social conflicts within a particular region. In the case of economics, an interest in culture is associated with an increasing interest in consumption and the awareness that trends cannot be explained satisfactorily in terms of a simple model of a rational consumer. In political science, despite the continuing dominance of the model of the rational voter, there is an increasing tendency to view politics as symbolic action and to study political communication in different media. Even hard-nosed analysts of world politics such as Samuel P. Huntington now speak of 'the clash of cultures' (see p. 2).[1]

In the case of history, some scholars who made their reputation writing political history, like John Elliott in his *Revolt of the Catalans* (1963), made a cultural turn, in Elliott's case by collaborating with an art historian, Jonathan Brown, in *A Palace for a King* (1980), a study of the building and decoration of the Buen Retiro palace near Madrid as a place to display the power of the Spanish Habsburgs. Historians are more likely today than in previous decades to use phrases such as 'print culture', 'court culture' or 'the culture of absolutism'. The following examples, taken from the titles of books published in the 1990s, may be sufficient to reveal the trend: 'the culture of merit', 'the culture of enterprise', 'the culture of gambling', 'the culture of life insurance', 'the culture of love', 'the culture of puritanism', 'the culture of absolutism', 'the culture of protest', 'the culture of secrecy' and 'the culture of politeness'. Even 'gun culture' has found its historian.[2] We are on the way to the cultural history of everything: dreams, food, emotions, travel, memory, gesture, humour, examinations and so on.

The slogan 'New Cultural History' (NCH) has been most successful in the USA, drawing together the literary historians associated with the 'new historicism' (see p. 41), art historians and historians of science, as well as what we might call 'plain' or 'ordinary' historians. However, the movement is an international one. In France, the phrase *histoire culturelle* has been slow to enter the language, thanks to rivals such as *l'histoire des mentalités* and *l'histoire de l'imaginaire social* (see p. 62), but Roger Chartier and others now define themselves as cultural historians. Chartier's *Cultural Origins of the French Revolution* (1990) was written as a response to Daniel Mornet's classic study, *The Intellectual Origins of the French Revolution* (1933), thus opposing a broader cultural to a narrower intellectual history.

In Germany and the Netherlands, NCH has been grafted onto the tradition of Burckhardt and Huizinga, giving a greater emphasis to the so-called 'history of the everyday'. In Britain, on the other hand, despite the presence of the Warburg Institute in London since the 1930s, cultural history is effectively a new development. As Keith Thomas remarked in 1989: 'In the UK there is no such subject. There are scarcely any chairs or lectureships in cultural history, no departments of cultural history, no journals of cultural history, no conferences on the subject.'[3] Although this situation is gradually changing, it is 'cultural studies' rather than cultural history that has risen to prominence in Britain in the last generation.

Cultural explanations

The expansion of the empire of culture includes an increasing propensity to offer cultural explanations for economic phenomena, the economic decline of Britain, for instance, or the wealth and poverty of nations in general. In 1961, John Elliott published an article called 'The Decline of Spain'; seventeen years later he published another article in the same journal, *Past and Present*, this time under the title 'Self-Perception and Decline in Early Seventeenth-Century Spain'. The shift from an interest in objective measures of decline to a greater concern with the sense of decline is characteristic of a generation of historians. In similar fashion, cultural explanations are offered more and more frequently for such changes in the political world as revolutions, state formation or even the Swedish intervention in the Thirty Years War.[4]

A striking example of a cultural explanation for political events comes from the work of a convert from political to cultural history, F. S. L. Lyons. In his last book, *Culture and Anarchy in Ireland, 1890–1939* (1979), Lyons described the country as divided into four cultures, those of the English, the Irish, the Anglo-Irish and the Ulster Protestants, four communities 'unable to live together or to live apart'. He argued that political problems were the relatively superficial manifestations of underlying cultural conflicts or 'collisions', and called for more attention to be given to cultural history, which in Ireland, he wrote, 'is still in its infancy'.

The contrast between the use of the term 'culture' by Lyons and by Matthew Arnold, whose title he adapted, is a revealing one. There has been a gradual shift in the use of the term 'culture' by historians in the last thirty years or so. Once used to refer to high culture, the term now includes everyday culture as well, in other words customs, values and a way of life. In other words, the historians have moved closer to the view of culture held by anthropologists (see p. 29).

The Moment of Historical Anthropology

Among the anthropologists who have been studied most carefully by historians are Marcel Mauss on the gift, Edward Evans-Pritchard on witchcraft, Mary Douglas on purity and Clifford Geertz on Bali. When Claude Lévi-Strauss was at the height of his fame, in the 1960s and 1970s, a number of historians were attracted by his structuralist approach, often to find that it resisted appropriation.

An early example of the anthropological turn comes from the USSR, as it then was. The Russian medievalist Aaron Gurevich is a specialist on Scandinavia. Trained as an agrarian historian, he became interested in conceptions of property in medieval Norway and Iceland. To make sense of a system based on the constant transfer of movable goods, he turned to anthropology.[5]

Gurevich compared the feasts of the Scandinavians with descriptions of the 'potlatch' among the Kwakiutl, an Indian people of British Columbia (the potlatch was a social occasion in which a chief would invite his equals and rivals to witness the destruction of valuable goods). He drew on Mauss's analysis of the rules of gift-giving in traditional societies, notably the obligation to receive and the obligation to repay, whether in the form of another gift (at a discreet interval) or in loyalty and services to the giver. In this way he explained the many references to gift-giving in the Icelandic sagas, concluding that in medieval Scandinavia generosity was not only a moral duty for important people and a condition of their status; it was also a quality with magical properties, producing peace and good harvests.

These conclusions can surely be extended to some other parts of Europe. In the case of Anglo-Saxon England, the political purposes of the feasts and the gifts of rings and weapons described so vividly in the epic poem *Beowulf* become clearer in the light of anthropological theory. More generally, the example of the anthropologists has encouraged historians to see the Goths, Vandals, Huns and other invaders of the Roman Empire in a more positive way, to attempt to reconstruct what might be called 'the civilization of the barbarians'.

The inspiration of Evans-Pritchard is apparent in the work of one of the pioneers of historical anthropology in Britain, Keith Thomas. For example, the chapters on astrology and witchcraft in Thomas's *Religion and the Decline of Magic* (1971), a study of early modern England, abound in references to Africa, such as the comparison of the English 'cunning folk' in Tudor and Stuart times to African diviners in the twentieth century. Thomas's analysis of the social function of the belief in witchcraft as a reinforcement of 'accepted moral standards' develops a suggestion first made by Evans-Pritchard, that the belief in witchcraft among the Azande (a Central African people) 'is a valuable corrective to uncharitable impulses, because a show of spleen or meanness or hostility may bring serious consequences in its train'.[6]

Mary Douglas, a pupil of Evans-Pritchard, also did fieldwork in Africa, but it was her general study *Purity and Danger* (1966) that attracted historians, especially the arresting theses that dirt 'exists in the eye of the beholder' and that it is a form of disorder. Thanks to this book, the long history of the western preoccupation with purity has become much more visible, in domains as different as language and the so-called 'infamous occupations' exiled to the margins of medieval cities and ranging from the physically dirty (dyeing cloth or tanning leather) to the morally impure (prostitutes and executioners).[7]

Purity and Danger was a central point of reference in a famous article by the American historian Natalie Davis on French riots during the Wars of Religion in the later sixteenth century. Davis viewed the wars 'from below' and observed the communal violence of the time, the lynching of Catholics by Protestants and of Protestants by Catholics, with anthropological eyes, interpreting the disturbances as a kind of ritual, 'rites of violence', and an attempt to purify the local community from the stain of heresy or superstition.[8]

While a few Anglophone historians were reading Evans-Pritchard and Douglas, some of their French colleagues were discovering the work of Claude Lévi-Strauss. What attracted their interest was not his more empirical work on the Indians of Brazil, such as the Bororo and the Nambikwara, but his general theory of culture, his so-called 'structuralism'. Lévi-Strauss had learned from the linguists to study the relations between the elements of a cultural or social system, focusing in particular on binary oppositions – high and low, light and dark, raw and cooked and so on.

Lévi-Strauss's four-volume study of Amerindian mythology appeared between 1964 and 1971, and inspired some historians, notably Jacques Le Goff and Emmanuel Le Roy Ladurie, to analyse European myths in a similar manner. Again, Keith Thomas's *Man and the Natural World* (1983) followed Lévi-Strauss in suggesting that the classification of animals in early modern England was a projection of the social structure onto nature.

A good example of a historical study that makes use of the insights of structuralism or semiotics, in the Russian rather than the French style, is Juri Lotman's essay on what he calls the 'poetics of everyday behaviour' in eighteenth-century Russia. Although he does not cite anthropologists, Lotman's essay makes the anthropological point that the more distant a culture is from us, the more easily we can treat its everyday life as an object of study. The advantage of choosing eighteenth-century Russia as a case-study is that the cultural westernization promoted by Peter the Great and his successors made the everyday problematic for Russian nobles, who needed manuals of conduct, like the *True Mirror of Youth* (1767), to tell them how to behave in a western manner. 'During and after the Petrine period, the Russian nobleman was like a foreigner in his own country', since ordinary people saw him as masquerading.[9]

Lotman treats the concept of a 'poetics' of everyday life as exceptional, limited to a certain period in Russian history, but this approach can be and has been employed more generally. Already in 1860, Jacob Burckhardt had made a case for an aesthetic approach to Renaissance politics and society, for viewing the state and society as 'works of art', while Stephen Greenblatt (see p. 41) offers a more general 'poetics of culture'.

The anthropologist who has inspired most cultural historians in the last generation, especially in the United States, is Clifford Geertz, whose 'interpretative theory of culture', as he calls it, is poles apart from the theory of Lévi-Strauss. Criticizing Edward Tylor's definition of culture as 'knowledge, belief, art, morals, law, custom' (see p. 35) on the grounds that it 'obscures a good deal more than it reveals', Geertz stresses meaning and what he called, in a famous essay with that title, 'thick description'. His own definition of culture calls it 'an historically transmitted pattern of meanings embodied in symbols, a system of inherited conceptions expressed in symbolic forms by means of which men communicate, perpetuate and develop their knowledge about and attitudes toward life'.[10]

What this means in practice becomes clearer if we look at Geertz's own ethnographies, notably his much-cited interpretation of the cockfight in Bali, in which he treats the sport as a 'philosophical drama', a key to the understanding of Balinese culture. The way in which Geertz links the cockfight to 'the wider world of Balinese culture' is not to view it as a 'reflection' of that culture. What he does instead is to treat the fight as a text, 'a Balinese reading of Balinese experience, a story they tell themselves about themselves', comparing it to *King Lear* or Dostoevsky's *The Brothers Karamazov* in our own culture. He describes the common practice of betting for high stakes on a cock's success as 'a dramatization of status concerns'. This is what makes the play 'deep'.[11]

It is not difficult to see what Geertz owes to the literary theorist Kenneth Burke, who was already expounding what he called the 'dramatistic approach' to culture in the 1940s. Another anthropologist who was thinking along similar lines to Geertz was Victor Turner, whose idea of a 'social drama', often employed by new cultural historians, developed out of his fieldwork in Africa, where he noted that disturbances in social life often passed through a 'more or less regular sequence', which could be divided into four phases: the breach of normal social relations, the crisis, the attempt at redressive action, and finally 're-integration', or alternatively, the recognition of 'schism'.[12]

Continuing this dramatistic or dramaturgical approach, Geertz went on to write a book about what he calls the 'theatre state' in nineteenth-century Bali. This was a state in which, according to the author, it is mistaken to assume, like many western political scientists, that ritual is a medium in the service of power. For the Balinese, as Geertz presented them, the reverse was the case: 'power served pomp, not pomp power'. The Balinese state may have been weak but it was spectacular. Its very *raison d'être* was spectacle.[13]

The impact of Geertz's work on cultural historians may be illustrated from Robert Darnton's book *The Great Cat Massacre* (1984). This is a collection of essays that grew out of a seminar on history and anthropology at Princeton in which Darnton and Geertz collaborated. Following the anthropologists, Darnton defined the task of the cultural historian as 'capturing otherness' and, following Geertz in particular, he suggested that 'one can read a ritual or a city, just as one can read a folktale or a philosophic text'. *The Great Cat Massacre* is a collection of such readings.

The book's title essay is concerned with an apparently trivial incident that took place in a printing shop in Paris in the 1730s. Annoyed by the howling of the local cats, which kept them awake at night, the apprentices working in the shop organized a hunt, followed by a mock trial of the cats and their 'execution' by hanging, to the delirious amusement of the organizers. At least this is how one of the apprentices remembered the incident in later life, when he wrote his memoirs.

Darnton begins his analysis with the laughter of the apprentices, suggesting that 'our own inability to get the joke is an indication of the distance that separates us from the workers of pre-industrial Europe'. To overcome this distance, he places the incident in a series of contexts, from labour relations to popular rituals and from attitudes to cats to views of violence. In this way he not only helps the reader to understand why the apprentices did what they did, but also makes the incident a point of entry into a lost world. One might say that he analyses the event as a 'social drama', even though he does not follow Turner's sequence.

This interpretation of the 'cat massacre' has been challenged, notably by Roger Chartier, who objects in particular to Darnton's conception of 'Frenchness', noting the paradox of emphasizing the cultural distance between the eighteenth century and the twentieth and stressing the continuity of a French cultural style. However, Chartier quotes Geertz himself with approval.[14]

Why has Geertz's work, and the essay on the cockfight in particular, made such an impact? His humanistic culture, his elegant prose and his defence of the interpretation of meanings (as opposed to the analysis of the social functions of customs, practised by so many of his anthropological colleagues in the 1960s and '70s) have all contributed to this warm reception. His concern with hermeneutics aligns him with the German tradition of cultural history. In any case, the 'drama analogy', as Geertz calls it, is an extremely powerful one, linking the older concern with 'high' culture to the new interest in the everyday. The power of this analogy helps explain the excitement generated not only by the work of Geertz and Turner but also by Erving Goffman's book, *The Presentation of Self in Everyday Life* (1959). For example, Goffman described a waiter who behaves in one way to the customers in the 'front region' of the restaurant, and in quite another way to his colleagues, in the kitchen, an area that might be described as 'backstage'.

The power of the drama analogy also helps to explain the growing historical interest in rituals. The tradition of studying official rituals such as coronations goes back to the 1920s, if not before, but in the 1960s and '70s historians such as Edward Thompson and Natalie Davis discovered popular rituals such as charivari, before they moved on to describe and analyse even more informal 'practices' and 'performances' (see p. 57), while the German scholar Richard van Dülmen studied early modern executions in his *Theatre of Horror* (1985).

An unusually sustained employment of the drama analogy can be found in Rhys Isaac's *The Transformation of Virginia* (1982), showing with particular clarity its value for cultural historians. Presenting his book as an example of 'ethnographic history', discussing his method in a long final chapter and taking the work of Goffman and Geertz as major points of reference, Isaac suggested that every culture has a distinctive 'dramaturgical kit' or repertoire.

In the case of Virginia, the idea of social life as a 'series of performances' is illustrated by emphasizing the 'ceremonial character' of meals in the Great House, tea-drinking, hospitality, courtroom procedures, elections, the mustering of the local militia, the adoption and signing of resolutions. The 'theatre model' is even used to interpret everyday micro-events such as the meeting between a white man and a slave, when the latter would put on 'an exaggerated show of submissiveness'.

However, the concern with anthropology on the part of historians, especially in Western Europe and the USA between the 1960s and the 1990s, went well beyond an interest in Geertz or social dramas. What was the reason for the increasing demand for anthropology at this time?

Encounters between disciplines, like encounters between cultures, often follow the principles of congruence and convergence. What attracts people from one culture to another is often an idea or a practice analogous to their own and so familiar and unfamiliar at the same time. Following this attraction, the ideas or practices of the two cultures come to resemble one another more closely. In the case we are discussing, we may say that the theory and practice of thick description helped a group of historians to move further in a direction in which they were already travelling. As the literary historian Stephen Greenblatt once put it, the encounter with Geertz's work 'made sense of something I was already doing, returning my own professional skills to me as more important, more vital and illuminating than I had myself grasped'.[15]

A number of the leading cultural historians of the later twentieth century – Emmanuel Le Roy Ladurie and Daniel Roche in France, for instance, Natalie Davis and Lynn Hunt in the USA, Carlo Ginzburg in Italy, Hans Medick in Germany – originally described themselves as social historians and admirers of Marx if not themselves Marxists. From the later 1960s onwards, they turned to anthropology in the search for an alternative way to link culture to society, one that did not reduce it to a reflection of society or a superstructure, the icing on the cake.[16]

The rise of interest in popular culture made anthropology even more relevant to historians. Anthropologists had already rejected the patronizing assumption that the people they studied did not understand their own cultures, and appreciated the local or unofficial knowledge of their informants.

The anthropologists' broad concept of culture was and remains another attraction, linking the study of symbols – once abandoned by plain historians to specialists on art and literature – to the everyday life that social historians were exploring. Part of the power of the drama analogy derives from its assistance in establishing such a link. The anthropological idea of cultural 'rules' or 'protocols' has also attracted cultural historians; the idea that – like children – they have to learn how things were done: how to ask for a drink, how to enter a house, how to be a medieval king or a Counter-Reformation saint.

It should not be forgotten that a few historians from older generations had already studied symbolism in everyday life. The best-known of these is surely Johan Huizinga, who drew, as we have seen, on the anthropology of his day in order to write his masterpiece on the late Middle Ages. In an autobiographical essay, Huizinga wrote that an early reading of Tylor's book, *Primitive Culture*, 'opened up perspectives which in a sense have inspired me ever since'.[17] Huizinga's *Autumn of the Middle Ages* described a religious man who used to cut his apples into three pieces in honour of the Trinity, and suggested that a meal at the court of Charles the Bold 'resembled the performance of a grand and solemn play'.

Before Huizinga, a Danish scholar, Troels Frederik Troels-Lund, inspired by the work of Scandinavian folklorists as well as German cultural historians, had discussed everyday symbolism in a series of fourteen volumes on *Daily Life in the North* (1879–1901), with sections on clothing, food and festivals.[18]

It was in 1953 that L. P. Hartley began his novel *The Go-Between* with the epigraph, 'The past is a foreign country. They do things differently there.' However, it was only in the 1970s that a group of historians began to quote Hartley and to claim that 'cultural history achieves most coherence and makes most sense when it is viewed as a kind of retrospective ethnography'.[19]

It is something of a paradox that it should have been via studies of remote peoples such as the Zande and the Balinese that western historians discovered the everyday symbolism on their doorstep, but as G. K. Chesterton and others have observed, it is often necessary to travel in order to see more clearly what we have at home. A hundred years ago, some Japanese came to value their own cultural heritage more highly when they became aware of western enthusiasm for wood-block prints, Noh plays and the music of the samisen.

The anthropological turn is also visible in the history of literature, art and science. Stephen Greenblatt, for example, has moved from the history of literature to what he calls 'the poetics of culture'. Like other literary historians in the group associated with the 'new historicism', a movement aimed at replacing literature in its historical or cultural context, Greenblatt's work has both developed from and turned against the Marxist tradition of 'literature and society'. In his *Shakespearean Negotiations* (1988), he rejected the traditional Marxian view of art as the reflection of society. Instead, he concentrated on what he called 'exchanges' or 'negotiations' between the two domains.

In an essay in that book entitled 'Shakespeare and the Exorcists', Greenblatt discussed the relation between two very different kinds of text, *King Lear* and the *Declaration of Egregious Popish Impostures*. The *Declaration* was an attack on the practice of exorcism and was published a short time before Shakespeare's play by the Protestant clergyman Samuel Harsnett. Harsnett's main argument against the exorcists was that they were really performing plays but hiding this fact from the audience. The central theme of the essay is what Greenblatt calls 'the transfer of possession and exorcism from sacred to profane representation'. He works with the 'drama analogy', but he also makes a contribution to its history.

Some scholars who used to describe themselves as art historians now say that they work on 'visual culture'. Two striking early examples of this turn towards visual culture come from the work of Bernard Smith and Michael Baxandall.

Smith's *European Vision and the South Pacific* (1959) argued that when Europeans (including the artists who accompanied the voyages of discovery) entered this region for the first time, they viewed Pacific peoples in a 'culture-bound' way, through the lens of the classical tradition or of stereotypes such as the noble savage. Tahitians, for instance, were viewed as a people living in the Golden Age, and Australian aborigines as Spartans or Scythians. The Antipodes was perceived as an inversion of Europe, a kind of world turned upside-down.

Again, Baxandall's *Painting and Experience in Fifteenth-Century Italy* (1972) discussed what the author calls the 'period eye', in other words the relation between the perception of paintings and everyday experiences ranging from dancing to gauging the contents of barrels. Baxandall's concern with 'a stock of patterns' is reminiscent of Aby Warburg (see p. 11), but his culturally relativist approach is equally reminiscent of anthropology, particularly the interpretative anthropology of Geertz, who in turn discussed Baxandall's book in one of his essays.

Historians of science have been moving in a similar direction, redefining themselves as cultural historians, as Nicholas Jardine and his colleagues do in a volume entitled *Cultures of Natural History* (1996). A recent study of the career of Galileo Galilei at the Medici court in Florence, Mario Biagioli's *Galileo Courtier* (1993) might be described as an example of historical anthropology.

Biagioli draws on Mauss and Malinowski in order to analyse the ties between Galileo and his patron, and on Geertz and Goffman to explain the pressures on the scientist to present himself and his discoveries in a dramatic fashion. For example, Galileo had to answer the questions that were put to him 'in a witty manner fitting the codes of court culture'. He was required to engage in disputes, sometimes at table after dinner, as a form of learned entertainment for his patron the Grand Duke. In the court environment of the early seventeenth century, 'what mattered was the show rather than the end product'.

It should be clear that some of the anthropological classics have proved to be very good for historians to think with and have offered solutions to some of their problems. All the same, it would be short-sighted to explain the rise of interest in anthropology purely in terms of the internal history of historical writing. Historians were reacting, consciously or unconsciously, to changes in the wider world, including the loss of faith in progress and the rise of anti-colonialism and feminism.

Under the Microscope

The 1970s witnessed the rise, or at least the labelling, of a new historical genre, 'micro-history', associated with a small group of Italian historians, among them Carlo Ginzburg, Giovanni Levi and Edoardo Grendi. This event might be viewed in at least three ways.

In the first place, micro-history was a reaction against a certain style of social history that followed the model of economic history, employing quantitative methods and describing general trends without communicating much sense of the variety or the specificity of local cultures. Second, micro-history was a response to the encounter with anthropology. Anthropologists offered an alternative model, that of an extended case-study in which there was space for culture, for freedom from economic or social determinism and for individuals, faces in the crowd. The microscope offered an attractive alternative to the telescope, allowing concrete individual or local experience to re-enter history.[20]

In the third place, micro-history was a response to a growing disillusionment with the so-called 'grand narrative' of progress, the rise of modern western civilization via ancient Greece and Rome, Christianity, the Renaissance, the Reformation, the Scientific Revolution, the Enlightenment and the French and Industrial Revolutions. This triumphalist story passed over the achievements and contributions of many other cultures, not to mention the social groups in the West that did not participate in the movements listed above. There is an obvious parallel between the critique of this grand narrative in history and the critique of the so-called 'canon' of great writers in English literature, or great painters in the story of western art. Behind these critiques may be seen a reaction against globalization, stressing the value of regional cultures and local knowledges.

Two books published in the middle of the 1970s put micro-history on the map: Emmanuel Le Roy Ladurie's *Montaillou* (1975) and Carlo Ginzburg's *Cheese and Worms* (1976), both of which combined academic success with an appeal to a much wider public.

Montaillou painted a historical portrait of a small French village in the Pyrenees and its two hundred-odd inhabitants at the beginning of the fourteenth century, a portrait made possible by the survival of the registers of the Inquisition, including interrogations of twenty-five villagers suspected of heresy. The book took the general form of a community study of the kind frequently made by sociologists, but the individual chapters raised questions that were being debated by French historians at this time, questions about childhood, for instance, about sexuality, the local sense of time and space or the peasant house as a representation of family values. *Montaillou* was a contribution to cultural history, in a wide sense that included material culture and mentalities.

Cheese and Worms was also based on Inquisition records, this time from sixteenth-century Friuli, in north-eastern Italy, and focused on the personality of one individual interrogated under suspicion of heresy, the miller Domenico Scandella, known as 'Menocchio'. To the surprise of the inquisitors, Menocchio answered their questions at great length, expounding his vision of the cosmos. The book owes its title to Menocchio's belief that in the beginning everything was chaos, the elements forming a mass 'just like cheese does in milk, and in that mass there appeared some worms, and those were angels'. In the course of his interrogation, Menocchio also spoke at length about the books he had read and the way in which he interpreted them. In this way Ginzburg's study contributed to the new 'history of reading' (see p. 60).

Cheese and Worms may be described as a 'history from below' because it concentrated on the world-view of a member of what the Italian Marxist Antonio Gramsci called the 'subaltern classes'. The book's hero, Menocchio, might be described as an 'extraordinary ordinary man', and the author explores his ideas from different angles, treating him sometimes as an eccentric individual who disconcerted his interrogators because he did not fit their stereotype of the heretic, and on other occasions as a spokesman for traditional, oral, peasant culture. The argument may not always be consistent, but it is always thought-provoking.

Other historical studies, inspired more by geography or folklore than by anthropology, have studied larger local units, the region rather than the village or the family. Charles Phythian-Adams, for example, has tried to identify what he calls the English 'cultural provinces', fourteen of them altogether, larger than counties but smaller than the customary divisions of England into the North-East, the Midlands, the South-West and so on. For his part, David Underdown has concentrated on variations in popular culture in the early modern period, relating cultural forms to the local economy and even to settlement patterns. He suggests, for instance, that football was especially popular in 'the Wiltshire and Dorset downlands, with their nucleated villages and sheep-corn economies'.[21]

Across the Atlantic, David Fischer's much-discussed *Albion's Seed* (1989) distinguished seven cultural regions in the USA today and four in colonial America, each of them shaped by migration from an English region, from East Anglia to Massachusetts, from the South of England to Virginia, from the North Midlands to the Delaware and finally, in the eighteenth century, from North Britain to the 'back country' west of Pennsylvania. Fischer argued that what he calls the 'folkways' – cultural traits ranging from language to types of housing – in each of the four regions were shaped by British regional traditions. The weather-boarded houses of New England, for instance, reproduced the houses of East Anglia, the accent and vocabulary of Virginians derived from the dialects of Sussex and Wessex, and so on.

Since the 1970s, hundreds of micro-historical studies have been published, focusing on villages and individuals, families and convents, riots, murders and suicides. Their variety is impressive but it is likely that these studies are subject to the law of diminishing intellectual returns to a given approach. The great problem – faced squarely by Ginzburg, though not by all his imitators – is to analyse the relation between the community and the world outside it. In his study of the Swabian village of Laichingen, for instance, the German micro-historian Hans Medick has placed particular emphasis on the relation between the local and the global.[22]

Postcolonialism and Feminism

As was suggested in the previous section, one major reason for the reaction against the grand narrative of western civilization was an increasing awareness of what it left out or made invisible. The struggle for independence in the third world and the debate about its continuing economic exploitation by the richer countries drew attention to the power of colonial prejudices and also their persistence into 'postcolonial' times. This was the cultural context for the rise of a theory of postcolonialism – or more exactly, competing theories – that later took the institutional form of 'postcolonial studies', an interdisciplinary cluster of topics including some cultural history.[23]

One of the books that did most to reveal the power of western prejudice was Edward Said's *Orientalism* (1978). This provocative study noted the importance of the binary opposition between Orient and Occident in western thought – describing it in terms that surely owe something to the example of Lévi-Strauss – and argued that this distinction between 'them' and 'us' was perpetuated by the academic specialists who should have undermined it, the professional Orientalists. Said also suggested that from the late eighteenth century onwards, Orientalism, whether manifest or latent, was implicated with colonialism and became 'a western style for dominating, restructuring, and having authority over the Orient'.

Orientalism analysed the various schemata through which the Middle East has been perceived by western travellers, novelists and scholars, stereotypes such as 'backwardness', 'degeneracy', 'despotism', 'fatalism', 'luxury', 'passivity' and 'sensuality'. It was an angry book, a passionate plea to foreigners to view Middle Eastern cultures without the blinkers of either hostility or condescension. It has inspired many similar studies, not only of Asia, Africa or the Americas, but of Europe as well. English views of Ireland have been labelled 'Celticism', while in an interesting counter-move, stereotypes of the 'West' have been termed 'Occidentalism'.[24]

Another struggle for independence, feminism, has had equally wide implications for cultural history, concerned as it has been both with unmasking male prejudices and with emphasizing the female contribution to culture, virtually invisible in the traditional grand narrative. For a survey of what has been done in this rapidly expanding field, one might turn to the five-volume *History of Women in the West* (1990–2) edited by the French historians Georges Duby and Michelle Perrot, which includes many essays on cultural history – on the education of women, for instance, on male views of women, female piety, female authors, books for women and so on.

For a case-study of the effects of feminist concerns on historical practice, we may turn to recent histories of the Renaissance. Although female scholars in particular had long been studying leading women of the Renaissance – Julia Cartwright's book on Isabella d'Este was published in 1903 – the article-manifesto by Joan Kelly, entitled 'Did women have a Renaissance?', became a landmark in the field by posing the problem in general terms.[25] In its wake a long series of studies of Renaissance women has appeared. One group of these studies concentrates on women artists of the period and the obstacles they encountered in the course of their careers. Another group of studies is concerned with female humanists from a similar perspective, noting how difficult it was for them to be taken seriously by their male colleagues or even to find time to study, whether they married or entered a nunnery.

Step by step, the addition of women to the field of study that we know as the Renaissance has led to its transformation or, as Kelly put it, its 'redefinition'.

For example, recent studies speak of 'women's writing' in the Renaissance, rather than 'literature', the point of the distinction being the need to look beyond the conventional genres of literature in which women are not well represented. Emphasis is now placed on what might be called 'informal forms' of writing such as private letters. Again, since women – Isabella d'Este, for instance – were more prominent as patrons of Renaissance art than as artists, the interest in women's history has encouraged the general shift of interest from production to consumption (see p. 68).[26]

For a case-study of the cultural history of women in the new style, we may turn to Caroline Bynum's *Holy Feast and Holy Fast* (1987), a study of the symbolism of food in the later Middle Ages, especially 'its pervasiveness in religious symbolism'. The author makes considerable use of the work of anthropologists such as Mary Douglas, Jack Goody and Victor Turner. She argues that food was a more important symbol for women than for men, 'an obsessive and overpowering concern in the lives and writings of religious women'. For instance, women 'thought of God as food' and were particularly devoted to the Eucharist. In this study, which is inspired by current debates over anorexia but carefully avoids projecting contemporary attitudes back onto the past, Bynum argues that female fasting was not pathological but meaningful. It was not only a form of self-control, but also 'a way of criticizing and controlling those in authority'.

It may be illuminating to compare and contrast this book with the chapters on religion in Huizinga's study of the late Middle Ages. Bynum places more emphasis on practice and more emphasis on women. She also expresses a more positive attitude to the proliferation of symbolism, which Huizinga took to be a sign of decadence. In these respects her book offers a fine example of the so-called 'new cultural history', the subject of the following chapter.

4
A New Paradigm?

The last chapter suggested that the encounter between historians and anthropologists inspired some of the most significant innovations in cultural history in the 1970s and 1980s. The marks on cultural history left by anthropology in general and Geertz in particular are still visible, but the so-called 'New Cultural History' has more than one source of inspiration. It is more eclectic at the collective as well as the individual level.

The phrase 'New Cultural History' (henceforward NCH) came into use at the end of the 1980s. A well-known book edited under this title by the American historian Lynn Hunt was published in 1989, but the essays collected in this volume were originally papers to a conference held in 1987 at the University of California at Berkeley on 'French History: Texts and Culture'. NCH is the dominant form of cultural history – some would even say the dominant form of history – practised today. It follows a new 'paradigm' in the sense that the term is used in the work of Thomas Kuhn on the structure of scientific 'revolutions', in other words a model for 'normal' practice out of which springs a tradition of research.[1]

The word 'new' serves to distinguish NCH – like the French *nouvelle histoire* of the 1970s, with which it has much in common – from the older forms already discussed. The word 'cultural' distinguishes it from intellectual history, suggesting an emphasis on mentalities, assumptions or feelings rather than ideas or systems of thought. The difference between the two approaches might be viewed in terms of Jane Austen's famous contrast between 'sense and sensibility'. The elder sister, intellectual history, is more serious and precise, while the younger is vaguer but also more imaginative.

The word 'cultural' also serves to distinguish NCH from another sister, social history. One domain in which a shift in approach is particularly visible is that of the history of cities. The political history of cities, 'municipal history', one might call it, has been practised since the eighteenth century, if not earlier. The economic and social history of cities took off in the 1950s and 1960s. The cultural history of cities is still more recent, a third wave made visible by Carl Schorske's book *Fin-de-SiècleVienna* (1979) and later studies. Schorske focuses on high culture but places it in an urban context. Other cultural historians are more concerned with urban subcultures, with the large city in particular as a stage offering many opportunities for the presentation or even the reinvention of the self.[2]

The new style of cultural history should be viewed as a response to the challenges outlined earlier (see chapter 3), to the expansion of the domain of 'culture' and to the rise of what has become known as 'cultural theory'. For example, the book by Caroline Bynum discussed at the end of the previous chapter is informed by the work of feminist theorists such as Julia Kristeva and Luce Irigaray who have analysed the differences between male and female discourse. Theory can be seen as a response to problems and as a reconceptualization of problems. Particular cultural theories have also made historians aware of new problems (or ones that they did not know they had), while creating new problems of their own.

A concern with theory is one of the distinctive features of the NCH. For example, the ideas of the German philosopher-sociologist Jürgen Habermas about the rise of the bourgeois 'public sphere' in eighteenth-century France and England have produced a shelf of studies criticizing and qualifying his ideas and also extending them to other periods, other countries, other social groups (women, for instance) and other domains of activity such as painting or music. The history of newspapers in particular has developed in response to Habermas's thesis.[3]

Again, Jacques Derrida's idea of the 'supplement', the role of the margin in the shaping of the centre, has been employed by historians in a number of different contexts. The American scholar Joan Scott has used the term to describe the rise of women's history, in which 'Women are both added to history' and 'occasion its rewriting' (as in the case of Renaissance women discussed in chapter 3). In similar fashion, a study of European witchcraft argues that in the early modern period, when many people felt threatened by witches, the belief system depended on precisely the element that they were attempting to exclude.[4]

Four Theorists

This section focuses on four theorists whose work has been particularly important for practitioners of the NCH: Mikhail Bakhtin, Norbert Elias, Michel Foucault and Pierre Bourdieu. I will summarize some of their key ideas before considering the ways in which they have been utilized. Bakhtin was a theorist of language and literature whose insights are also relevant to visual culture, while the other three were social theorists working at a time when the boundaries between society and culture seemed to be dissolving (see p. 29). The point of discussing the theorists here is not to persuade readers to accept their ideas and simply apply them to the past, but to encourage them to test the theories and in so doing to investigate new historical topics or to reconceptualize old ones.

The voices of Mikhail Bakhtin

Mikhail Bakhtin, one of the most original cultural theorists of the twentieth century, was discovered by historians, outside Russia at least, following the translation into French and English of his book *Rabelais and his World* (1965). Within Russia, he was one of the inspirations for the so-called 'Tartu school' of semiotics, which included Juri Lotman (see pp. 35–6). The basic concepts employed in the Rabelais book – 'carnivalization', for instance, 'uncrowning', 'the language of the marketplace' and 'grotesque realism' – have been employed so frequently in the NCH that it is difficult to remember how we ever managed without them.

For example, in a new and illuminating approach to the history of the German Reformation and its effect on the popular culture of the time, Bob Scribner made use of Bakhtin's work on Carnival and on rituals of desacralization, arguing that mock-processions, for instance, were used by the reformers as a dramatic way of showing ordinary people that Catholic images and relics were inefficacious.

From sixteenth-century France, these ideas have migrated to eighteenth-century England, and from the history of literature to the history of art (to studies of Brueghel, for instance, or of Goya). As for Bakhtin's view of the importance of the subversion and penetration of 'high' culture by 'low', especially by popular laughter, it is – or at any rate was – in danger of becoming a new orthodoxy, accepted without criticism.[5]

By contrast, the equally interesting ideas put forward by Bakhtin about speech genres and about the different voices that can be heard in a single text – what he calls 'polyphony', 'polyglossia' or 'heteroglossia' – have attracted relatively little attention outside the literary world. This is a pity, since it is surely illuminating to approach Carnival, for example, as the expression of a number of different voices – playful and aggressive, high and low, male and female – rather than reducing it to a simple expression of popular subversion.

Again, in an age in which the idea of a solid or unitary self is challenged, the idea of heteroglossia is of obvious relevance to the study of what some historians call 'ego-documents', in other words texts written in the first person. A diary that includes extracts from newspapers or a travel journal that incorporates passages from guidebooks make obvious examples of the co-existence, if not the dialogue, between different voices.

The civilization of Norbert Elias

Norbert Elias was a sociologist with a lifelong interest in history and a lifelong concern with both 'culture' (literature, music, philosophy and so on) and 'civilization' (the art of everyday living). His *Civilizing Process* (1939), discussed in chapter 1, was a contribution to social theory as well as to history.

Among the central concepts of this study was 'the threshold of embarrassment' (*Schamgrenze*) and 'the threshold of repugnance' (*Peinlichkeitschwelle*). According to Elias, these thresholds were gradually raised in the seventeenth and eighteenth centuries, thus excluding more and more forms of behaviour from polite society. Another basic concept is the 'social pressure for self-control' (*Soziale Zwang nach Selbstzwang*). An outer ring of concepts includes 'competition', 'habitus', a term made famous later by Bourdieu (see pp. 56–7) and 'figuration', the ever-changing pattern of relations between people, compared by Elias to a dance.

First published in German in Switzerland in 1939, *The Civilizing Process* evoked little interest at the time, but from the 1960s onwards it has been increasingly influential, on historical anthropologists such as Anton Blok, cultural historians such as Roger Chartier, and even on art historians and historians of science. The increasing use of the term 'civility' in the work of English-speaking historians is an indicator of the growing awareness of the importance of Elias, even if knowledge of his work is virtually restricted to his studies of the court and the dining-table, omitting his work on sport, on time or on the contrast between the established and the outsiders.

The Civilizing Process has also been the object of a number of criticisms, for virtually dismissing the Middle Ages, for instance, for failing to say more about Italy or about sex, and for overestimating the influence of courts and underestimating that of cities. The author's apparent assumption that 'civilization' was a fundamentally western phenomenon has also come to seem extremely odd. One might sum up the reaction of cultural historians to the ideas of Elias by saying that they are often critical of his interpretation of history, but have come to find his social and cultural theory very good to think with.

The regime of Michel Foucault

Where Elias stressed self-control, Foucault emphasized control over the self, especially control over bodies exercised by the authorities. Foucault, first a philosopher turned historian and then a historian of ideas turned social historian, gained his reputation with a series of books on the history of madness, clinics, intellectual systems, surveillance and sexuality.[6] So far as the NCH is concerned, three of the ideas he launched have been particularly influential.

In the first place, Foucault was a sharp critic of teleological interpretations of history in terms of progress, evolution or the rise of freedom and individualism put forward by Hegel and other nineteenth-century philosophers and often taken for granted in the everyday practice of historians. His approach in terms of 'genealogy', a term he took from Nietzsche, stressed the effects of 'accidents' rather than tracing the evolution of ideas or the origins of the present system.

Foucault also stressed cultural discontinuities or 'ruptures', for example the change in the relationship between words and things around the middle of the seventeenth century, the 'invention' of madness in the seventeenth century and of sexuality in the nineteenth. In all these cases, what Kuhn would call a new 'paradigm' replaced an earlier one relatively quickly. The stress on cultural construction in recent contributions to the NCH, to be discussed below, owes a good deal to Foucault.

In the second place, Foucault regarded systems of classification, 'epistemes' or 'regimes of truth', as he called them, as expressions of a given culture and at the same time forces shaping that culture. He called himself an 'archaeologist' because he believed that the work of historians was superficial and that it was necessary to dig deeper in order to reach intellectual structures or, as he preferred to call them, 'networks' (*réseaux*) and 'grids' (*grilles*). The point of the 'grid', like that of the intellectual 'filter', was to suggest that structures admit some information while excluding the rest.

In the inaugural lecture *The Order of Discourse* (1971) following his appointment to a chair in 'the history of systems of thought' at the Collège de France, Foucault defined his aim as the study of the control of thought, including the ways in which certain ideas or topics are excluded from an intellectual system. Three out of his four major substantive studies are concerned with the exclusion of certain groups (mad people, criminals and sexual deviants) from the intellectual and social orders that they were perceived to threaten.

By contrast, *The Order of Things* (1966) dealt with the categories and the principles underlying and organizing whatever could be thought, said or written in a given period, in this case the seventeenth and eighteenth centuries, in other words the 'discourses' of the period. In this work Foucault suggested that these collective discourses, rather than individual writers, were the proper object of study, shocking some readers but inspiring others. Foucault's concept of discourse was one of the principal inspirations for Said's *Orientalism* (see pp. 46–7). The problem for would-be followers of Foucault is that this central notion of discourse, like Kuhn's notion of paradigm or Marx's notion of class, is an ambiguous one. To make the point crudely, how many discourses were there in eighteenth-century France? Three, thirty or three hundred?

In the third place, Foucault wrote an intellectual history that included practices as well as theories and bodies as well as minds. His concept of practices is linked to an emphasis on what he called the 'microphysics' of power, in other words politics at the micro-level. 'Discursive practices', he claimed, construct or constitute the objects spoken about, and ultimately culture or society as a whole, while 'the gaze' (*le regard*) was an expression of the modern 'disciplinary society'.

In *Discipline and Punish* (1975), the author presented a series of parallels between prisons, schools, factories, hospitals and barracks as so many institutions for the production of 'docile bodies'. The spatial organization of classrooms, for instance, like that of parade-grounds and shop-floors, facilitated control by means of surveillance. In a famous passage, he described the nineteenth-century reformer Jeremy Bentham's plan for an ideal prison, the 'Panopticon', designed so that the authorities would be able to see everything while remaining invisible themselves.

The uses of Pierre Bourdieu

Unlike Elias and Foucault, Bourdieu, a philosopher turned anthropologist and sociologist, did not write history himself, although he had a good knowledge of history and made many perceptive observations about nineteenth-century France. However, the concepts and theories that he produced in the course of his studies, first of the Berbers and then of the French, are of great relevance for cultural historians. They include the concept of 'field', the theory of practice, the idea of cultural reproduction and the notion of 'distinction'.[7]

Bourdieu's concept of a 'field' (*champ*) – literary, linguistic, artistic, intellectual or scientific – refers to an autonomous domain that achieves independence at a particular moment in a given culture and produces its own cultural conventions. So far, the idea of a cultural field has not attracted many historians, although scholars concerned with French literature and the rise of the intellectual have found the concept to be an illuminating one.

More influential has been Bourdieu's theory of what he calls 'cultural reproduction', the process by which a group such as the French bourgeoisie maintains its position in society via an educational system that appears to be autonomous and impartial, while in fact selecting for higher education students with the qualities inculcated from birth in that social group.

Another important contribution of Bourdieu is his 'theory of practice', especially his concept of the 'habitus'. Reacting against what he considered to be the rigidity of the idea of cultural rules in the work of structuralists such as Lévi-Strauss, Bourdieu examined everyday practice in terms of sustained improvisation within a framework of schemata inculcated by the culture in mind and body alike (the terms he used included *schéma corporel* and *schème de pensée*). He borrowed the term 'habitus' from the art historian Erwin Panofsky (who had in turn taken it from the scholastic philosophers) to refer to this capacity for improvisation.[8] In

France, for example, according to Bourdieu, the bourgeois habitus is congruent with the qualities prized and privileged in the system of higher education. For this reason, the children of the bourgeoisie succeed in examinations, appearing to do so quite 'naturally'.

Bourdieu made much use of a master metaphor drawn from economics, analysing culture in terms of goods, production, the market, capital and investment. His phrases 'cultural capital' and 'symbolic capital' have passed into the everyday language of sociologists, anthropologists and at least some historians.

Bourdieu also employed the military metaphor of 'strategy', not only in his analysis of peasant marriages but in his studies of culture as well. When the bourgeoisie is not investing its cultural capital to the best advantage, it is employing strategies of distinction, making use of the music of Bach or Stravinsky, for instance, as a means of differentiating itself from groups it views as 'inferiors'. As Bourdieu puts it: 'Social identity lies in difference, and difference is asserted against what is closest, which represents the greatest threat.'

As in the case of Elias, it is not the relatively abstract field theory or theory of reproduction that has attracted cultural historians so much as Bourdieu's trenchant observations on bourgeois styles of life, especially the search or the battle for 'distinction'. Yet the general theory also has something to offer historians who wish to analyse as well as to describe. The theory has been criticized as too determinist or reductionist, but it forces us to re-examine our assumptions about both tradition and cultural change.

Together, all four theorists have encouraged cultural historians to concern themselves with both representations and practices, the two distinctive features of NCH, according to one of its leaders, Roger Chartier.

Practices

'Practices' is one of the slogans of NCH: the history of religious practice rather than theology, the history of speaking rather than the history of linguistics, the history of experiment rather than of scientific theory. Thanks to this turn towards practices, the history of sport, once left to amateurs, has become professionalized, a field with its own journals such as the *International Journal for the History of Sport*.

Paradoxically enough, the history of practices is one of the domains of recent historical writing that has been most affected by social and cultural theory. From the perspective of practices, Norbert Elias, whose concern with the history of table manners once seemed eccentric, is now firmly in the mainstream. Bourdieu's work on distinction has inspired many studies of the history of consumption, while Foucault's idea of a disciplinary society in which new practices were adopted to ensure obedience has been adapted to study other parts of the world.

In *Colonising Egypt* (1988), for instance, Timothy Mitchell draws on both Foucault and Derrida in his discussion of the cultural consequences of nineteenth-century colonialism. From Foucault, Mitchell has learned to discuss the European 'gaze' and to look for parallels between developments in domains as different as the army and education, focusing in both cases on the importance of discipline. From Derrida comes the idea of meaning as 'the play of difference', central to a chapter on the effect of printing, introduced around the year 1800, on the practice of writing.

The history of language, more especially the history of speech, is another field which a cultural history of practices is beginning to colonize, or more exactly to share with sociolinguists who have been feeling the need for a historical dimension to language studies. Politeness is one speech domain which has attracted cultural historians, while insult has attracted still more.[9]

Religious practice has long been a concern of historians of religion, but the increasing body of work on meditation and pilgrimage (Hindu, Buddhist, Christian or Muslim) suggests a change of emphasis. The pilgrimage to Lourdes, for example, has been replaced in its political context by Ruth Harris as a national movement of penance that began in the 1870s as a response to French defeat in the Franco-Prussian war. Under the influence of anthropologists such as Victor Turner (see p. 37), pilgrimages have been studied as rituals of initiation and as liminal phenomena. The participants are viewed as suspended between their everyday world and the world they wish to enter, abandoning their normal social roles and status and merging themselves in the pilgrim community.[10]

Travel history is yet another example of the history of a practice which is undergoing a kind of boom, marked by the foundation of specialist journals such as the *Journal of Travel Research* as well as by the publication of ever more monographs and collective volumes. Some of these studies are especially concerned with the art or method of travel, the rules of the game. Treatises on this topic were published in Europe from the later sixteenth century onwards, advising their readers to copy epitaphs in churches and graveyards, for instance, or to enquire into the forms of government and the manners and customs in the places they visited.[11]

The history of practices is making an impact on relatively traditional fields of cultural history such as the study of the Renaissance. Humanism, for instance, used to be defined in terms of the key ideas of the humanists, such as their belief in the 'dignity of man'. Today, it is more likely to be defined in terms of a cluster of activities such as copying inscriptions, attempting to write and speak in the style of Cicero, purifying classical texts from the corruptions introduced by generations of copyists or collecting classical coins.

Collecting is a form of the history of practices which appeals to art historians, historians of science and the staff of galleries and museums. *The Journal of the History of Collections* was founded in 1989 and a number of important studies of 'cabinets of curiosities', museums and art galleries also appeared in that decade. The main focus is on what has been described as 'the culture of collecting'. Scholars have studied what was collected (coins, shells and so on), the philosophy or psychology of collecting, the organization of collections, their basic categories (the theory underlying the practice) and finally the accessibility of the collections, which were generally privately owned before the French Revolution but have become increasingly public since that time.[12]

As a case-study in this field, it may be illuminating to leave the West for Ming China, as described by Craig Clunas in his book *Superfluous Things* (1991). The title of this study comes from the *Treatise on Superfluous Things* written in the early seventeenth century by the gentleman scholar Wen Zhenheng.

The point is that a concern with the superfluous is a sign that one can afford not to be concerned with the necessary, in other words that one belongs to an elite, a 'leisure class'.

Wen's treatise forms part of a Chinese tradition of books on connoisseurship, discussing themes such as how to distinguish genuine antiques from false ones or how to avoid vulgarity (typified for example by tables ornamented with wooden dragons). Drawing on Bourdieu, Clunas argues that 'The constant assertion of difference between things in the *Treatise* is nothing more nor less than an assertion of the difference between people as consumers of things', particularly the difference between the scholar-gentry and the new rich.

The turn towards the history of everyday practices is even more obvious in the history of science, which used to be viewed as a form of intellectual history but is now more concerned with the meaning of activities such as experimenting. Attention has been displaced from heroic individuals and their great ideas towards the changing methods of what Thomas Kuhn called 'normal science', finding a place in the story for the contributions of the craftsmen who made the scientific instruments and the laboratory assistants who actually carried out the experiments.[13]

The history of reading

One of the most popular forms of the history of practices is the history of reading, defined against the history of writing on the one hand, and on the other against an earlier 'history of the book' (the book trade, censorship and so on). The cultural theory of Michel de Certeau (discussed below, pp. 76–8), underlies the new focus on the role of the reader, on changes in reading practices and on the 'cultural uses' of print. Historians of reading such as Roger Chartier originally proceeded on parallel lines to the literary critics concerned with the 'reception' of works of literature, but after some years the two groups have become aware of each other.[14]

Responses to texts by individual readers, studied through their marginalia and underlinings, or in the case of Ginzburg's Menocchio, discussed above (see pp. 44–5), through interrogations by the Inquisition, have become a popular topic of research. For example, the many letters written by readers to Jean-Jacques Rousseau after the publication of his novel *La Nouvelle Héloise* have been studied by Robert Darnton. This early example of fan-mail is full of references to the tears provoked by the novel. There is also a body of work on female readers and their tastes in books. John Brewer has analysed the diary – which extends to seventeen volumes – of an eighteenth-century Englishwoman Anna Margaretta Larpent, noting 'her predilection for women authors and for works with female protagonists'. It has been argued that the rise in the eighteenth century of the history of manners and customs and the 'history of society', including the history of women, at the expense of political and military history, was in part a response to the increasing feminization of the reading public.

Current topics of interest and debate within the history of reading in the West include three apparent changes or shifts: from reading aloud to silent reading; from reading in public to reading in private; and from slow or intensive reading to rapid or 'extensive' reading, the so-called 'reading revolution' of the eighteenth century.

As the increasing number of books made it impossible for any individual to read more than a fraction of the total, so the argument goes, readers reacted by devising new tactics such as skimming or skipping or consulting the contents or the index in order to suck information out of a volume without reading it from cover to cover. The emphasis on a sudden change is probably exaggerated, and it is more likely that readers made use of more than one of these different reading styles according to the book or the occasion.[15]

That the years around 1800 were nevertheless a watershed in the history of reading, at least in Germany, has been argued in a highly original study which examines – among other topics – changes in lighting, furniture and the organization of the day (divided more clearly than before into hours of work and hours of leisure), as well as the rise of a more empathetic mode of reading, especially in the case of works of fiction.[16]

Historians of East Asia and historians of the twentieth century are also turning to the history of reading, adapting the approach to study Japanese writing systems and literary genres, for example, or the impact of the rise of the market on the Russian system of book production in the 1990s.[17]

Representations

On one occasion Foucault criticized historians for what he called their 'impoverished idea of the real', which left no space for what is imagined. Since then, a number of leading French historians have responded to this provocation. One famous example of this kind of history is the French historian Georges Duby's *Three Orders* (1978), a study of the circumstances surrounding the rise of the famous medieval image of society as composed of 'three estates': those who pray, those who fight and those who work (or plough) – in other words the clergy, the nobility and the 'third estate'. Duby presents this image not as a simple reflection of the medieval social structure, but rather as a representation with the power to modify the reality it appears to mirror.

Another contribution to the history of what the French call *l'imaginaire social* (the social imagination, in other words whatever is imagined, rather than the purely imaginary) is Jacques Le Goff's *Birth of Purgatory* (1981). Le Goff explains the rise of the idea of purgatory in the Middle Ages by relating it to changing ideas of space and time. Le Goff was also one of the scholars who launched the history of dreams in the early 1970s, inspired by studies of dreaming by sociologists and anthropologists.[18] Studies of visions and ghosts have also been encouraged by the new concern for the active role of the imagination, emphasizing the creative combinations of elements from paintings, stories and rituals.[19]

In English, by contrast, the phrase 'the history of the imagination' has not yet established itself, despite the success of Benedict Anderson's 1983 study of nations as 'imagined communities' (see pp. 82–3). A more common term is 'the history of representations'.

So many forms of representation, whether literary, visual or mental, have been studied in the last two or three decades that even a bare list might swell this section into a chapter. There are histories of representations of nature, like Keith

Thomas's *Man and the Natural World* (1983), which charts changes in English attitudes between 1500 and 1800, stressing the 'revolution' that displaced humans from the centre of the natural world and the rise of a love of animals and of wild nature.

Again, there are histories of representations of the social structure, like Duby's three estates; representations of labour, including working women; representations of women as goddesses, whores, mothers or witches; and representations of the 'Other' (of Jews by Gentiles, of whites by blacks and so on). Literary and visual images of the saints became a major focus of interest within the history of Catholicism in the 1980s. As an early student of the subject observed: 'Sanctity, more perhaps than anything else in social life, is in the eye of the beholder.'[20]

Representations is the title of an interdisciplinary journal founded at Berkeley in 1983. Among the first contributions to the journal were articles by the literary critic Stephen Greenblatt on images of sixteenth-century German peasants, by the art historian Svetlana Alpers on Foucault's reading of a painting by Velázquez, and by the historians Peter Brown (on saints), Thomas Laqueur (on funerals) and Lynn Hunt (on the 'crisis of representations' in the French Revolution).

In the literary field, Said's *Orientalism* is essentially concerned with representations of the so-called 'Other', particularly images of the 'East' in the West. Again, studies of the history of travel often focus on the stereotyped ways in which an unfamiliar culture is perceived and described, and on the 'gaze' of the traveller, distinguishing imperial, female, picturesque and other kinds of eye. It can be shown that some travellers had read about the country before they ever set foot in it, and on arrival they saw what they had learned to expect.

Vivid examples of stereotyping come from accounts of Italy written by foreign travellers in the seventeenth and eighteenth centuries, repeating commonplaces about the *lazzaroni* of Naples, for example, poor men lying in the sun and apparently doing nothing. The topos of the world turned upside-down has appealed to travellers from the days of Herodotus onwards as a way of organizing their observations. For example, the Scottish Puritan Gilbert Burnet, Bishop of Salisbury, viewed the Italy through which he travelled in the

1680s as a land of superstition, tyranny, idleness and popery, in other words exactly the opposite of the enlightenment, freedom, industriousness and Protestantism that he attributed to Britain.

Orientalism in music

For a case-study in the history of representations we may turn to musicology, another discipline in which some practitioners now define themselves as cultural historians. The way in which some musicologists have responded to Said's *Orientalism*, a study written by a literary critic and inspired by a philosopher, offers a vivid illustration of interdisciplinary contacts or 'negotiations' under the capacious umbrella of cultural history.

Art historians responded to Said's book in the 1980s, historians of music in the 1990s. Even Said himself, despite his enthusiasm for opera, waited until 1993 to make his own contribution in this area, a discussion of Verdi's *Aida* in which he suggests that the opera confirmed the western image of the Orient as 'an essentially exotic, distant and antique place in which Europeans can mount certain shows of force'.[21]

Two recent studies take this theme further by pointing to its complexities. Ralph Locke's study of Saint-Saëns's *Samson et Dalila* notes that the world of the Bible was identified with the nineteenth-century Middle East, allowing the composer to give his opera some local colour, or more exactly local sound. Saint-Saëns presents the Other – especially the female other, Delilah – in the conventional manner as both terrifying and seductive, but he also gives her a great romantic aria, thus subverting 'the characteristically Orientalist binarism of this opera's plot'.[22]

Again, Richard Taruskin's study of musical Orientalism in nineteenth-century Russia turns on a paradox. Evocations of exotic music such as Borodin's 'In the Steppes of Central Asia' or Mussorgsky's 'Dances of the Persian Slave Girls' assumed a binary opposition between the Russian and the Oriental (male and female, master and slave). When Diaghilev took some of this music to Paris, however, the French public took these oriental sounds to be typically Russian.[23]

The history of memory

Another form of the NCH that is currently enjoying a boom is the history of memory, sometimes described as 'social memory' or 'cultural memory'. Academic interest in the topic was both revealed and encouraged by the publication between 1984 and 1993 of seven volumes edited by the French scholar-publisher Pierre Nora under the title *Les Lieux de mémoire* and concerned with the 'national memory' in France as it has been maintained or reshaped by books such as Larousse's encyclopaedia, by buildings such as the Panthéon, by practices such as the annual commemoration of the taking of the Bastille on 14 July, and so on.[24] By contrast there has been much less research to date on the more elusive but arguably no less important topic of social or cultural amnesia.

Similar multi-volume collective projects to Nora's have since been published in Italy, Germany and elsewhere. As films and television programmes reveal even more clearly than books, there is a strong popular interest in historical memories. This increasing interest is probably a reaction to the acceleration of social and cultural change that threatens identities by dividing what we are from what we were. At a more specific level, the rise of interest in memories of the Holocaust and the Second World War comes at a time when these traumatic events are on their way out of living memory.

Like the history of travel, the history of memory is a domain which reveals with unusual clarity the importance of schemata or stereotypes, already underlined by the psychologist Frederick Bartlett in his book *Remembering* (1932). As events recede, they lose something of their specificity. They are elaborated, usually unconsciously, and so come to resemble the general schemata current in the culture, schemata that help memories to endure at the price of distorting them.

Take the case of the Protestants of the South of France, for instance, studied by a historian who is one of them, Philippe Joutard. Joutard shows how, in a culture steeped in Scripture, memories of the persecution of the Protestant community by Catholics were contaminated or even shaped by biblical stories of the persecution of the Chosen People, down to the marks made on the doors of houses whose inhabitants were to be massacred. Reading Joutard's account, it is difficult not to think of the Holocaust, a traumatic event that is also remembered within a biblical framework, since the term 'holocaust' means 'burnt offering'.[25]

Again, British memories of the miseries of the trenches of the First World War were shaped by recollections of John Bunyan's *Pilgrim's Progress*, a book that was still widely read at the time. As the American critic Paul Fussell has put it, 'front-line experience seemed to become available for interpretation when it was seen how closely parts of it resembled the action of *Pilgrim's Progress*', as the mud of the trenches resembled the Slough of Despond. By contrast, memories of the Second World War were shaped by knowledge of the First.[26]

These examples of the effect of books – probably books read aloud in a group – on the process of remembering are remarkable ones, but of course memories are not transmitted or shaped by reading alone. Ireland today, North and South, is famous, or some would say notorious, for the power of memories of past events, reinforced by the trauma of civil war, evoked by places such as Drogheda and Derry and re-enacted in the annual parades of Orange lodges and the Ancient Order of Hibernians. On the walls of Belfast, graffiti exhort the passer-by to 'Remember 1690'.

In this Irish context, Geertz's famous remark about the 'story they tell themselves about themselves' looks problematic (see p. 36). Catholics and Protestants do not tell themselves the same stories. One side erects statues, the other blows them up, following what has been described as 'a well-established tradition of explosive de-commemoration'. The memories of conflict are also conflicts of memory.[27]

Within each religious community, Geertz's remark may still be valid, but it remains necessary to ask the great social question, 'Whose memory are we talking about?'. Men and women, the older generation and the younger, may not remember the past in the same way. In a given culture, one group's memories may be dominant and other's subordinate, as in the case of the winners and the losers of a civil war – in Finland in 1918, for instance, or Spain in 1936–9.

Material Culture

Cultural historians have traditionally paid less attention to material culture than to ideas, leaving the material realm to the economic historians. The pages that Norbert Elias devoted to the history of the fork and the history of the handkerchief in his book on the civilizing process were unusual for their time. For their part, economic historians used to neglect the symbolic aspects of food, clothes and shelter, looking instead at levels of nutrition or the amount of an individual's income that was spent on different commodities. Even Fernand Braudel's famous study of the early modern world, *Civilization and Capitalism* (1979), or, to use his own phrase, *civilisation matérielle*, may be criticized – and has been criticized – on these grounds, despite its importance as a comparative analysis of the movement of objects between different culture areas.

In the 1980s and '90s, however, some cultural historians turned to the study of material culture, and so found themselves associating with the archaeologists, museum curators and specialists in the history of costume and furniture who had long been working in this area. Historians of religion, for example, have been paying more attention to changes in church furnishings as indicators of changes in religious attitudes. In the 1960s, the British social historian Asa Briggs wrote books on *Victorian People* and *Victorian Cities*. In 1988, his cultural turn was revealed by the publication of *Victorian Things*, although the book had been planned long before.

Even historians of literature have turned in this direction, studying graffiti or comparing sonnets to miniatures as private tokens of love, while the New Zealander Don McKenzie, who redefined bibliography as a form of cultural history in his *Bibliography and the Sociology of Texts* (1986), emphasized the need to study the 'material forms of books', 'the fine detail of typography and layout', arguing that non-verbal elements including 'the very disposition of space' were conveyers of meaning. In the language of the theatre, another enthusiasm of McKenzie's, we might say that the physical appearance of the printed page functions as a series of cues to readers, encouraging them to interpret the text in one way rather than another.

Most studies of material culture stress the classic trio of topics – food, clothes and housing – often focusing on the history of consumption and the place of the imagination, played upon by advertising, in stimulating the desire for goods. The relation between today's 'consumer culture' and the interest in past consumption is obvious enough, but historians in this field are generally well aware of the dangers of anachronism.

An exemplary contribution to the history of food was made by the American anthropologist Sidney Mintz in *Sweetness and Power: the Place of Sugar in Modern History* (1985). Mintz's history is both social and cultural. It is social in its concern with the consumer and the transformation of sugar from a luxury for the rich to a staple item of the everyday consumption of ordinary people, whether taken in coffee or tea. On the other hand, *Sweetness and Power* is cultural in its concern with the symbolic aspect of sugar. This symbolic power was greatest when sugar was a luxury that distinguished its consumers from the mass of the population, but as the commodity moved down the social ladder it was given new meanings and incorporated in new social rituals.

In *The Culture of Clothing* (1989) the French historian Daniel Roche turned to the history of clothes on the grounds that it 'tells us much about civilizations'. Dress codes reveal cultural codes. 'Behind the apparel', Roche remarks, 'I believe that you really can find mental structures.' In eighteenth-century France, for instance, conforming to a particular dress code was a way for an individual to show that he or she was noble, or to attempt to pass for noble. A choice of clothes was a choice of role in what the historian calls the 'sartorial theatre' of the epoch. Roche goes on to make a connection between the 'clothing revolution' and the French Revolution, viewed as the rise of 'liberty, equality and frivolity'. He takes frivolity seriously because the attention to clothing in the feminine press in the later eighteenth century implied that fashion was 'no longer the preserve of the privileged'.[28]

As a case-study of the history of housing, one might take the Swedish anthropologist Orvar Löfgren's history of the bourgeois home in nineteenth-century Sweden in *Culture Builders* (1979), a book which combined the traditional Scandinavian ethnography in which Löfgren and his co-author Jonas Frykman were trained with ideas taken from Elias and Foucault. *Culture Builders* noted the shift from 'austerity' to 'opulence' in the later nineteenth century, arguing that the change took place because the home 'became the stage on which the family paraded its wealth and displayed its social standing'. The furniture and interior decoration, especially in the drawing-room, supported the self-presentation of the family to the visitors. Readers who remember the image of the Ekdahl family home in Uppsala around 1900, as it was represented in Ingmar Bergman's film *Fanny and Alexander* (1982), will have no problem visualizing these forms of opulent display, which had their parallels in Britain, France, Central Europe and elsewhere at this time.

However, the bourgeois home in what the Swedes call the 'Oscar period' (1880–1910) was not only a stage but also a 'sanctuary', a refuge from the increasingly impersonal society outside. Hence the increasing importance of private rooms such as the bedroom and the nursery, and the increasingly sharp distinction between public and private spaces within the house.

The reference to the spaces of the home is worth noting. It may appear somewhat paradoxical to include space within 'material culture', but cultural historians, like historians of architecture and historical geographers before them, are coming to read the 'text' of a city or a house between the lines. The history of cities would be incomplete without studies of marketplaces and squares, just as the history of housing would be incomplete without studies of the use of space in the interiors.

Some of the theorists discussed earlier in this chapter, from Habermas on coffee-houses as locales of political discussion to Foucault on the layout of schools and prisons as an aid to discipline, have helped draw the attention of historians to the importance of space – sacred and profane, public and private, masculine and feminine and so on.

Historians of science now concern themselves with the spaces within laboratories or anatomy theatres, while historians of empire study the layout of the cantonment and the bungalow. Art historians look at galleries and museums as spaces as well as institutions, historians of drama study theatres, music historians examine the design of opera houses and concert halls, while historians of reading pay attention to the physical organization of libraries.

The History of the Body

If there is one domain of the NCH that is flourishing today but would have seemed almost inconceivable a generation earlier – in 1970, say – it is the history of the body.[29] The few contributions that had been made to it in earlier decades were little known or considered as marginal.

For example, from the 1930s onwards, the Brazilian sociologist-historian Gilberto Freyre studied the physical appearance of slaves, as recorded in advertisements for information about runaways published in nineteenth-century newspapers. He noted the references to the tribal marks that revealed the part of Africa the slaves had come from, to the scars from repeated whippings, and to the signs of work, such as the loss of hair by men who carried heavy loads on their heads. Again, a study published in 1972 by Emmanuel Le Roy Ladurie and two collaborators used military records to study the physique of nineteenth-century French conscripts, noting, for instance, that they were taller in the North and shorter in the South, a difference in height almost certainly due to differences in nutrition.[30]

From the early 1980s, on the other hand, a growing stream of studies has been concerned with male and female bodies, with the body as experience and as symbol, with dismembered bodies, anorexic bodies, athletic bodies, dissected bodies and the bodies of saints and sinners. The journal *Body and Society*, founded in 1995, is a forum for historians as well as sociologists. Books have been devoted to the history of bodily cleanliness, of dancing, of drill, of tattooing, of gesture. The history of the body developed out of the history of medicine, but historians of art and literature as well as anthropologists and sociologists have become involved in what might be called this 'bodily turn' – had there not been so many turns already that readers may be in danger of becoming dizzy.

Some of the new studies may best be described as claiming new territory for the historian. The history of gesture is an obvious example. The French medievalist Jacques Le Goff opened up the subject; an international group of scholars, ranging from classicists to art historians, have contributed to it, while Le Goff's former pupil Jean-Claude Schmitt has devoted a major work to gesture in the Middle Ages. Schmitt notes the increasing interest in the topic in the twelfth century, which left behind a corpus of texts and images that has enabled him to reconstitute religious gestures such as praying and feudal gestures such as dubbing a knight or doing homage to a lord. He argues, for instance, that praying with joined hands (rather than extended arms) and also kneeling to pray were transfers to the religious domain of the feudal gesture of homage, kneeling before one's lord and placing one's hands within his.[31]

An example from Russian history may show the importance of paying historical attention to apparently small differences. In 1667, the Russian Orthodox Church was split into two, when a church council, meeting in Moscow, supported recent innovations and excommunicated the supporters of tradition, who were later known as the Old Believers. One of the issues in this debate was whether the gesture of blessing should be made with two fingers or three. It is not difficult to imagine how later rationalist historians have described these debates, viewing them as typical of the religious or superstitious mind, remote from real life and unable to distinguish the significant from the insignificant. However, that minor gesture implied a major choice. Three fingers meant following the Greeks, two fingers meant retaining Russian traditions. To quote Bourdieu yet again, 'Social identity lies in difference'.

Other studies in the history of the body also challenge traditional assumptions. For example, Peter Brown's *The Body and Society* (1988) has helped to undermine the conventional view of the Christian hatred of the body. So has Caroline Bynum's *Holy Feast and Holy Fast* (1987), discussed above (see p. 48), as an example of women's history, but equally important for its discussion of the body and its food as a medium of communication.

As one of the pioneers in the field, Roy Porter, has observed, the rapid rise of interest in the subject was doubtless encouraged by the spread of AIDS, which drew attention to 'the vulnerability of the modern body'. The rise of interest in the history of the body also runs parallel to interest in gender history (see p. 47). However, the references to the body in the theorists discussed at the beginning of this chapter suggest a deeper explanation for a more gradual trend. For example, Mikhail Bakhtin's discussion of medieval popular culture had much to say about grotesque bodies and especially about what the author described as 'the material lower bodily stratum'. A concern with the body was implicit, if not always explicit, in Norbert Elias's history of self-control.

In the work of Michel Foucault and Pierre Bourdieu, the philosophical underpinnings of the study of the body become visible. Like the French philosopher Maurice Merleau-Ponty, Foucault and Bourdieu broke with the philosophical tradition going back to Descartes that separated the body from the mind, the idea of 'the ghost in the machine' as the English philosopher Gilbert Ryle mockingly described it. Bourdieu's concept of habitus was expressly designed to bridge the gap or to avoid the simple opposition between minds and bodies.

Revolution in cultural history?

In this chapter I have tried to give readers some idea of the variety of approaches practised under the umbrella of the NCH. The collective achievement of the last two or three decades is a considerable one, and the movement is even more impressive when viewed as a whole. If there have been few innovations in method, in the strict sense of the term, many new topics have been discovered and explored with the aid of new concepts.

All the same, continuities with earlier scholarship should not be forgotten. The NCH developed out of the historical anthropology discussed in chapter 3 and some of its leading figures, from Natalie Davis to Jacques Le Goff or Keith Thomas, belong to both movements.

Again, the Swiss architect Sigfried Giedion wrote a pioneering study of material culture, *Mechanisation takes Command* (1948), in which he argued that 'for the historian there are no banal things', since 'tools and objects are outgrowths of fundamental attitudes to the world'. The phrase 'collective representations' was used more than a century ago by the sociologist Emile Durkheim, followed in the 1920s by Marc Bloch. The interest in 'schemata' noted at several points in this chapter goes back to Aby Warburg and Ernst-Robert Curtius (see p. 11).

The similarities between certain recent trends and some of the work of Burckhardt and Huizinga also deserve emphasis. Warburg and Huizinga already saw the relevance of anthropological studies of so-called 'primitive' peoples to the history of classical antiquity and the Middle Ages. Clifford Geertz is an admirer of Burckhardt and refers to his work from time to time, while Darnton, in his years as a crime reporter, read Burckhardt's *Civilization of the Renaissance* in the office, so he tells us, concealed between the pages of *Playboy*: 'And I still think it is the greatest history book I have ever read.'[32]

Despite these palpable continuities, it would be hard to deny that a collective shift or turn in the theory and the practice of cultural history has taken place in the course of the last generation. The shift might be viewed as a change of emphasis rather than the rise of something quite new, a reform of tradition rather than a revolution, but after all, most cultural innovation takes place in this way.

The NCH has not gone unchallenged. The theory underlying it has often been criticized and rejected, not only by traditional empiricists but also by innovative historians such as Edward Thompson, in a tirade entitled 'The Poverty of Theory' first published in 1978. The traditional anthropological concept of culture as 'a concrete and bounded world of beliefs and practices' has been criticized on the grounds that cultures are the site of conflicts and only 'loosely integrated'.[33]

An even more controversial theory underlying much of the NCH is that of the cultural construction of reality, to be discussed in the following chapter.

5
From Representation to Construction

It was suggested earlier in the book that solutions to problems eventually generate problems of their own. Take the idea of 'representation', for instance, a central concept in the NCH. It seems to imply that images and texts simply reflect or imitate social reality. However, many practitioners of the NCH have long been uncomfortable with this implication. Hence it has become common to think and speak of the 'construction' or the 'production' of reality (of knowledge, territories, social classes, diseases, time, identity and so on) by means of representations. The value and the limitations of this idea of cultural construction deserve to be discussed in some detail.

In a well-known epigram, Roger Chartier has spoken of a recent shift 'from the social history of culture to the cultural history of society'. He offers this formula as a description of certain 'displacements' of interest on the part of historians in the 1980s, notably the shift away from social history in the 'hard' sense of the study of social structures such as social classes. The idea of the 'cultural history of society' reveals the influence on the NCH of the movement of 'constructivism' in philosophy and other disciplines, from sociology to the history of science.[1]

The Rise of Constructivism

It was the philosophers and scientists who began to challenge received opinions about objective knowledge. Albert Einstein, for instance, declared that it is our theory that decides what we can observe, and Karl Popper agreed (see p. 12).

The German philosopher Arthur Schopenhauer had already argued that 'the world is my representation' (*Die Welt ist meine Vorstellung*), while Friedrich Nietzsche claimed that truth is created rather than discovered. Nietzsche also described language as a prison, while Ludwig Wittgenstein asserted that 'the limits of my language are the limits of my world'. The American philosophical movement known as pragmatism moved in a similar direction. John Dewey, for instance, claimed that it is we who create reality, that each individual constitutes his or her world out of the encounter between self and environment. William James argued that 'Mental interests ... help to make the truth which they declare'.[2]

If it was once possible, indeed normal, for historians to ignore Nietzsche or Wittgenstein, it has become increasingly difficult to evade discussions of the problematic relation between language and the outside world it was once supposed to 'reflect'. The mirror has been broken. Doubt has been cast on the assumption that a representation 'corresponds' with the object represented. The assumption of transparency dear to traditional scholars has been challenged. Historical sources now appear to be more opaque than we used to think.

Ironically enough, it is not difficult to suggest social explanations for the turn to 'constructivism' in the later twentieth century. The rise of 'history from below', for example, as in the case of Edward Thompson's *Making of the English Working Class* (see p. 18) involved an attempt to present the past from the point of view of ordinary people. So did the rise of the history of the colonized in Asia, Africa and America, which emerged together with postcolonial studies and has often focused on 'the vision of the vanquished' or the point of view of the 'subaltern classes'.[3] In similar fashion, feminist historians have tried not only to make women 'visible' in history, but also to write about the past from a female point of view. Hence historians have become increasingly aware that different people may view the 'same' event or structure from very different perspectives.

It is in this context that cultural historians, together with sociologists, anthropologists and other scholars, have become involved in what used to be seen as a purely philosophical or scientific debate. The question whether, or, better, the extent to which or the ways in which, scholars construct their objects of study has itself turned into a major object of study. It is a special case of what some philosophers and sociologists call the 'social construction of reality'.

Psychologists, for example, increasingly present perception as an active process rather than a reflection of what is perceived. Linguists write less about language as a reflection of social reality and more about speech 'acts' and their effects. Sociologists, anthropologists and historians speak more and more of the 'invention' or 'constitution' of ethnicity, for instance, of class, or of gender or even of society itself. In the place of the former sense of constraints, of social determinism, of a world of 'hard' social structures, many scholars now express an almost dizzying sense of freedom, of the power of the imagination, of a world of socio-cultural forms which are 'soft', malleable, fluid or fragile. Hence the title of a recent book by the sociologist Zygmunt Bauman, *Liquid Modernity* (2000).

Re-employing Michel de Certeau

One influential formulation of the 'constructivist' position was offered by Michel Foucault in his *Archaeology of Knowledge* (1969) when he defined 'discourses' as practices that 'systematically construct (*forment*) the objects of which they speak'. This definition illustrates the trend that was already being described as the 'linguistic turn' in the 1960s, though the phrase has become much more common since. However, constructivists owe even more to the cultural theory of Michel de Certeau, formulated a few years later.[4]

Michel de Certeau was a many-sided man who can equally well be described as a theologian, philosopher, psychoanalyst, anthropologist or sociologist. He identified himself primarily as a historian, and made important contributions to the history of mysticism, historiography and language. His study of a notorious seventeenth-century case of the possession by devils of a group of nuns in the small French town of Loudun made extensive use of the 'drama analogy' discussed in chapter 3, writing of the event as 'spectacle' and of 'the theatre of the possessed'. The book he wrote about the linguistic policies of the French Revolution took a subject that historians had previously neglected and demonstrated its political and cultural importance.[5]

So far as the NCH is concerned, however, Certeau's most influential study is not one of his historical works but rather the book on everyday life in France in the 1970s that he and some collaborators published in 1980.[6] Where earlier sociologists studied what they generally called the 'behaviour' of consumers, voters and other groups, Certeau preferred to speak about 'practices', *pratiques*. The practices he analysed were those of ordinary people; everyday practices such as shopping, walking a neighbourhood, arranging the furniture or watching television. One reason for his referring to 'practices' rather than 'behaviour' was to ensure that his readers would take the people he wrote about as seriously as they deserved.

Where earlier sociologists had assumed that ordinary people were passive consumers of mass-produced items and passive spectators of television programmes, Certeau, by contrast, emphasized their creativity, their inventiveness. He described consumption as a form of production. He emphasized the choices that individuals made from the mass-produced objects displayed in the shops and the freedom with which they interpreted what they read or saw on the television screen. His concern with creativity is highlighted by the original French title of his book, 'the invention of the everyday', *L'invention du quotidien*.

More precisely, identifying a particular kind of invention, Certeau wrote of 'uses', 'appropriation' and especially of 're-employment' (*ré-emploi*). In other words, he was thinking in terms of ordinary people making selections from a repertory, making new combinations between what they select and, not least, placing what they had appropriated in new contexts. This construction of the everyday through practices of re-employment is part of what Certeau calls 'tactics'. The dominated, so he suggested, employ tactics rather than strategies because they have a restricted freedom of manoeuvre within the limits set by others. They have, for example, the freedom to 'poach', Certeau's famous metaphor for creative forms of reading that turn official meanings into subversive ones.

There are obvious similarities between the ideas of Certeau and those of some of his contemporaries, notably Foucault and Bourdieu, with whom he entered into dialogue. He inverted Foucault, replacing the concept of discipline by that of 'anti-discipline'. His notion of 'tactics', expressing a view from below, was put forward in deliberate opposition to Bourdieu's 'strategy', which emphasized the view from above. Certeau's key idea of 'practice' has much in common with that of Bourdieu, but he criticized the notion of habitus for its implication that ordinary people are unconscious of what they are doing.

The reception of literature and art

Certeau is a major figure, though not the only one, in a major shift in studies of art, literature and music in the last generation, the shift from a concentration on artists, writers and composers to a concern with the public as well, with their responses, their 'reception' of the works they saw, heard or read.

This shift has already been illustrated from the history of reading (see chapter 4). In art history too there is a steady flow of monographs written from this point of view. For example, David Freedberg's important book *The Power of Images* (1989) concentrates on religious responses, linking certain kinds of image to the rise of meditative practices in the late Middle Ages and early modern times. Meditation on the Passion of Christ, a favourite topic of devotional works of the time, was assisted by paintings such as Mathias Grünewald's *Crucifixion* or the many cheap woodcuts that circulated from the fifteenth century onwards. Freedberg also studies iconoclasm (in Byzantium, in the Netherlands in 1566, in France in 1792 and so on) as a form of violence that reveals the values of the perpetrators, especially a belief, conscious or unconscious, in the power of images.

The invention of invention

If Foucault and Certeau are right about the importance of cultural construction, then all history is cultural history. A list of all the historical studies published since 1980 with the words 'invention', 'construction' or 'imagination' in their titles would certainly be both long and various. It would include studies on the invention of the self, Athens, the barbarian, tradition, the economy, the intellectual, the French Revolution, primitive society, the newspaper, the Renaissance woman, the restaurant, the Crusades, pornography, the Louvre, the people and George Washington.

Take the case of illness, for example. The new cultural history of the body is distinguished from the more traditional history of medicine by its emphasis on the cultural construction of illness, more especially 'madness'. Michel Foucault introduced this perspective in the work that made his reputation, *Madness and Civilization* (1961). In Britain, Roy Porter's *Mind-Forged Manacles* (1990) was a landmark, criticizing the psychiatrist Thomas Szasz for suggesting that the 'manufacture of madness' was a kind of plot, and suggesting instead that in different periods there were different 'cultures of madness', perceptions of abnormality and stereotypes of mad people such as fools and melancholics.

A substantial number of recent studies of this kind focus on the invention of nations, Argentina, for instance, Ethiopia, France, Ireland, Israel, Japan, Spain and Scotland (though not, so far as I know, of England). There are also studies of the cultural construction of regions – Africa, the Balkans, Europe, Eastern Europe, the North of Europe (Scandinavia) and the North-East of Brazil (Pernambuco, Bahía and neighbouring states).

New Constructions

The past itself is viewed by some scholars as a construction, notably by the American Hayden White. In *Metahistory* (1973) White's aim was to offer what he called a 'formalist' analysis of historical texts, concentrating on nineteenth-century classics such as Jules Michelet, Leopold von Ranke,

Alexis de Tocqueville and Jacob Burckhardt. The author claimed that each of the four great nineteenth-century historians modelled his narrative or 'plot' on that of a leading literary genre. Thus Michelet wrote, or to use White's own term, 'emplotted', his histories in the form of romance, Ranke in that of comedy, Tocqueville in that of tragedy and Burckhardt in that of satire.

White was developing some ideas on plot in historical writing that were originally put forward by the Canadian critic Northrop Frye. In an essay of 1960 in which he also used the term 'metahistory', Frye took as his starting point the famous reflections of Aristotle on the difference between poetry and history.[7] However, he did introduce a major qualification: 'When a historian's scheme gets to a certain point of comprehensiveness', he wrote, 'it becomes mythical in shape', and he offered Edward Gibbon and Oswald Spengler as examples of historians whose plots were tragic, concerned as they were with the decline of the Roman Empire and the decline of the West.

One might say that White began where Frye left off, playing down the Aristotelian contrast between poetry and history and extending the idea of plot to historical works in general. He stands on the border between two positions, or propositions, the conventional view that historians construct their texts and interpretations, and the unconventional view that they construct the past itself.

White's book and the other essays in which he develops his position have been extremely influential. His term 'emplotment' has entered the discourse of a number of historians, whether their object of study is a particular historical writer or contemporary views of political conflict.

Constructing class and gender

Social categories, once treated as if they were firm and fixed, now appear to be flexible and fluid. Historians and anthropologists working on India no longer take the category 'caste' for granted. On the contrary, they treat it as a cultural construct with a history, a political history linked to that of imperialism. Something similar has happened to the concept of 'tribe', which historians and anthropologists studying Africa have become increasingly reluctant to use in their own work.[8] 'Ethnicity', a term in much more general use today than it was a generation ago, is a social category often regarded as flexible or even negotiable.

'Class' too, which was once treated as an objective social category by Marxists and non-Marxists alike – however they might disagree over its definition – is now increasingly regarded as a cultural, historical or discursive construct. Edward Thompson's *Making of the English Working Class*, for instance, has been criticized for assuming that experience translates itself into consciousness without the mediation of language. As Gareth Stedman Jones puts it, 'Consciousness cannot be related to experience except through the inter-position of a particular language which organizes the under-standing of experience', a language that he set out to analyse in the case of the English Chartists.[9]

Feminists have been encouraging historians and others to treat 'gender' in the same way. As we noted in chapter 2 (p. 28), it is necessary to distinguish between male views of femininity (experienced by females as pressures on them to behave in particular ways, 'modestly', for example), from female views current at the same time and social level. The latter are enacted all the time in everyday life in the process of 'doing gender'.

In other words, returning to the dramaturgical model, masculinity and femininity are increasingly studied as social roles, with different scripts in different cultures or sub-cultures, scripts that are originally learned at the mother's – or father's – knee, however they may be modified later through the influence of peer-groups, conduct-books, and a variety of institutions including schools, courts and factories. These scripts include posture, gesture, language and clothes, not to mention forms of sexual behaviour. In Renaissance Italy, for example, men were permitted to make dramatic ges-tures, but respectable women were not. Too much movement of the hands suggested that a woman was a courtesan.

Models of masculinity and femininity are often defined by contrast – the manly Englishman, for instance, against the effeminate Frenchman or 'Oriental'. Another point empha-sized in recent work is the interdependence of models of masculinity and femininity in a given culture. Each is defined relative to the other, or even against the other.

This point emerges clearly from a study by Patricia Ebrey, *The Inner Quarters* (1993), concerned with China under the Tang dynasty (960–1279). In this period she identifies 'a general shift in ideals of manhood', away from the warrior and towards the scholar. Hunting was replaced by collecting antiques as a fashionable pursuit for high-status males. Pierre Bourdieu, whose ideas on 'distinction' have already been discussed (see pp. 56–7) would have appreciated the possibility that the shift towards scholarship was prompted by the desire of the Chinese to distinguish themselves from their warlike neighbours such as the Turks and Mongols.

At about the same time, ideals of womanhood also changed. Women were increasingly seen as beautiful, passive, delicate and fragile, like the flowers to which poets compared them. The same period saw the rise of the practice of foot-binding. Ebrey suggests that all these changes were linked. More specifically, 'Because the ideal upper-class man was by Sung times a relatively subdued and refined figure, he might seem effeminate unless women could be made even more delicate, reticent and stationary'.

Constructing communities

The year 1983 may be taken as a symbolic date in the making of constructivist history, at least in the English-speaking world, since it was the year of publication of two extremely influential books, one written by Benedict Anderson and the other a collective volume edited by Eric Hobsbawm and Terence Ranger.

Anderson's *Imagined Communities* is the work of a specialist on South-East Asia with global interests and a global vision. The book has made a contribution to the abundant literature on the history of modern nationalism that is distinctive in at least three respects. In the first place, in its perspective, since the author chose to look at Europe from outside and devotes much of his space to the history of Asia and the Americas. In the second place, the book was unusual in its time in its cultural approach to politics. The author identified the roots of what he called 'the culture of nationalism' not in political theory but in unconscious or semiconscious attitudes to religion, time and so on.

A third distinctive feature of Anderson's essay is his emphasis on the history of the imagination, summed up in his felicitous and successful phrase 'imagined communities'. He had much to say about the place of printed matter, especially newspapers, in the construction of new imagined communities such as nations in the place of older ones such as Christendom. Anderson did not seem to be aware of the turn to *l'histoire de l'imaginaire social* on the part of French historians a little before him, but he moved in a similar direction. He resembles these historians in admitting the power of the collective imagination, or of shared images, in making things happen. Although he did not use the term 'construction', he assumed the importance of this process.

By contrast, the idea of construction is central to Hobsbawm's and Ranger's *The Invention of Tradition*, a provocative re-examination of one of the central concepts in cultural history. This volume of essays grew out of a conference organized by the Past and Present Society, and the conference in turn grew out of an idea of Eric Hobsbawm's about the special importance of the period 1870–1914 for the production of new traditions. The volume includes a series of illuminating case-studies of England, Wales, Scotland and the British Empire in India and Africa, dealing with the rise of the kilt and the leek and especially with new forms of royal or imperial ritual. Hobsbawm's introductory essay amplified the impact of these studies by putting forward a general argument – subversive at the time – to the effect that traditions 'which appear or claim to be old are often quite recent in origin and sometimes invented'.

The Invention of Tradition helped renew one of the most traditional forms of cultural history, the history of tradition itself, yet its reception seems to have surprised everyone. The volume was much more successful than either the editors or the publishers (Cambridge University Press) originally expected. The value of Hobsbawm's hypothesis about the late nineteenth century has been emphasized by the authors of studies of many other parts of the world, from Japan to Brazil. In the course of this warm reception, however, the message of the book was reinterpreted. Its organizing idea was taken to mean that all traditions are invented. Today, Hobsbawm's introductory remarks, quoted above, seem not so much subversive as conservative, given his use of the qualifiers 'often' and 'sometimes' and his warning that 'the strength and adaptability of genuine tradition' should not be confused with invention.

In another way, though, Hobsbawm was an accurate prophet, since he noted the special relevance of the concept 'invention of tradition' to nations and nationalisms. 'Nation' is now regarded as a paradigm case of construction; witness the shelf of books mentioned above with the word 'invention' in their titles.

By what means does this invention and construction take place? A number of recent studies have stressed the contribution of political festivals to the construction of community from medieval coronations to the parades of the Orange lodges in Northern Ireland on 12 July. These collective actions not only express but also reinforce the participants' sense of collective identity.

More unusual is Simon Schama's account of 'the creation of Dutch nationhood' in the seventeenth century in *The Embarrassment of Riches* (1987). The Dutch were a new nation, which came into existence in the course of a revolt against Philip of Spain. They were a group in search of a collective identity. They found or made what they were looking for, in part by identifying themselves with the ancient Batavians, who had fought the Roman Empire as the Dutch were fighting that of Spain, and with the Israelites, who had declared their independence from Pharaoh's Egypt.

To these points, already made by Dutch historians, Schama added one of his own. Inspired by the work of Mary Douglas on purity discussed in chapter 3, he interpreted the seventeenth-century Dutch obsession with cleanliness, on which so many foreign travellers remarked (not always in a complimentary fashion), as 'an affirmation of separateness'. In the language of Freud, Dutch cleanliness illustrates the 'narcissism of minor differences', the point that 'it is precisely the minor differences in people who are otherwise alike that form the basis of feelings of estrangement or hostility between them'. In the language of Pierre Bourdieu, it exemplifies the search for 'distinction'. In the language of the British anthropologist Anthony Cohen, it reveals the 'symbolic construction of community'.[10]

The construction of monarchy

Three studies published in the 1990s on Russia, Japan and France may serve to illustrate the shift from representation to construction in the political domain.

Richard Wortman's *Scenarios of Power* (1995) studied the place of myth and ceremony in the making of the Russian monarchy. The author drew on cultural theory, from Geertz to Bakhtin, and although he did not cite Goffman, he revealed a Goffmanesque sensitivity to the ubiquity of drama, at least in the court and its environment. The book centres on the idea of 'scenario', including the scenarios of conquest, domesticity, dynasty, enlightenment, friendship, happiness, humility, love, nationality and reform. Coronations, weddings, funerals, religious processions and military parades are all viewed as confirmations of power or demonstrations of national unity.

Takashi Fujitani's *Splendid Monarchy: Power and Pageantry in Modern Japan* (1996) is concerned with the invention of tradition in Japan after the imperial restoration of 1868. The author suggests that 'Japan's governing elites invented, revived, manipulated and encouraged national rituals with unprecedented vigour' at this time, as part of a policy of involving ordinary people in 'the culture of the national community' and making them aware that they were the object of the imperial gaze. Particularly important were the pageants and processions on the occasion of imperial accessions, weddings, funerals and progresses through the provinces. Fujitani argues that these progresses 'produced power simply by their pomp and glitter, not because they communicated any particular myth or ideology'. As in the case of Russia, the use of exotic foreign items such as English coaches enhanced the effect. Inspired by Foucault, Fujitani discusses the 'imperial gaze', noting that people were afraid to look up at the emperor but were aware that he was watching them.

It is not always clear where individual historians stand on the question of the discursive construction of social reality. For this reason I have chosen to discuss one of my own books, *The Fabrication of Louis XIV* (1992). As in the case of the tsars, we see in the case of Louis the ritualization or even the theatricalization of much of his everyday life. The king's daily rising and going to bed, the *lever* and the *coucher*, were organized as a kind of ballet (a genre that Louis appreciated and in which he sometimes performed). Royal meals of different degrees of formality may also be viewed as so many performances before a selected audience. They were 'scenarios', in Wortman's sense.

Take the case of the institution known as 'the apartments' (*les appartements*). Following his move to Versailles in 1682, Louis opened some of his rooms in the palace to the nobility three times a week for billiards, cards, conversation and refreshments. One point of the innovation was to introduce a degree of informality into Versailles. All the same, it is scarcely stretching the term too much to describe these occasions as 'rituals', since they were devised to communicate a message. They were a means of affirming the king's accessibility to his subjects (an accessibility that was also marked by the striking of a medal). In practice, Louis soon failed to make an appearance, but the theatre of accessibility continued to run for a long time.

It is difficult to know quite how much of the king's daily life to include under the rubric of 'ritual'. For this very reason, examining the life of Louis offers an opportunity to reflect on both the value and the limitations of this concept. Here, as elsewhere, it might be more illuminating to refer to activities as more or less ritualized (more or less stereotyped, more or less symbolic) rather than to describe ritual as a separate class of action.[11] After all, contemporary observers claimed that even the king's slightest gestures were rehearsed.

In the analysis of everyday life in Versailles, the work of Goffman (see p. 38) shows its value once again. The king was always on stage when he was present in the 'front regions' of the palace. However, the royal study or *cabinet* may be described as 'backstage'. Here the king was alone with Madame de Maintenon, once his mistress but later his wife (as everyone knew but no one dared mention in public).

A vivid contemporary description of the management of the transition from the back region to the front has survived, noting how Louis composed himself and tried to look dignified as he went through the doorway separating his private from his public sphere. By this means the king contributed to the creation of an ideal image of himself that helped maintain the power of the monarchy.

Besides representing himself in this way, Louis was represented in many sculptures, paintings and engravings as well as poems, histories and periodicals (including the official *Gazette*). These texts and other objects allow historians to write about what used to be called the public 'image' of the king, a topic that has interested scholars ever since the rise of advertising at the end of the nineteenth century made us image-conscious.

I chose to refer to the fabrication of Louis XIV rather than to the fabrication of his image not only because the shorter title is more dramatic, but also to make the point that the king was continuously created or recreated through the performances in which he played his role – the 'great role', as a Swedish historian called it in a study of King Gustav III.[12] The performances and the many representations of those performances – representations of representations – made Louis visible to different audiences: to his nobles, to his people, to foreign courts and even to posterity. These representations became reality in the sense of affecting the political situation. However, they were not the only reality. Some contemporaries recorded their awareness of discrepancies between the public image of the king as a warrior, for instance, and the actual behaviour of Louis, who preferred to keep his distance from the battlefield.

In the context of constructivism, it may be interesting to note the opposite reactions to my book. Some traditional historians were surprised that I took the image of Louis so seriously as to write a book devoted entirely to this theme rather than to discussing the king's policies. On the other hand, some postmodern readers seemed unhappy with the suggestion that there was something outside the text, a real individual behind the representations. These days, cultural historians have to walk a tightrope.

Constructing individual identities

A concern with the construction of identity is a major feature of the NCH, unsurprisingly enough in an age in which 'identity politics' has become a major issue in so many countries. Increasing interest is taken in personal documents or, as the Dutch say, 'ego-documents'. These are texts written in the first person, whether they take the form of letters, of the travelogues discussed earlier (see p. 59), or of diaries and autobiographies, including the autobiographies of artisans, tinkers for instance, tailors, cobblers, carpenters, or the glass-maker Jacques-Louis Ménétra of Paris, whose remarkable account of his life during the French Revolution was discovered by Daniel Roche.[13]

There is an increasing concern with the rhetoric of these documents, 'the rhetoric of identity'. Letters, for example, were written according to conventions that varied according to the epoch, the social position of the writer and also the kind of letter being written (the familiar letter between equals, the begging letter from inferior to superior and so on).

For example, in her book *Fiction in the Archives* (1987), Natalie Davis studied what she called 'Pardon Tales and their Tellers in Sixteenth-Century France'. In these stories of homicide in 'hot anger', self-defence and so on, and petitions for pardon written to the king – probably by lawyers on behalf of their clients – what interests Davis is what she calls the 'fictional' aspects of these documents. As she explains: 'By "fictional" I do not mean their feigned elements, but rather, using the other and broader sense of the root word *fingere*, their forming, shaping and moulding elements: the crafting of a narrative.'

As in the case of the pardon tales, the traditional view of autobiographies as either telling the truth or lying has gradually been replaced by a more subtle approach that takes into account the conventions or rules for self-presentation in a given culture, the perception of the self in terms of certain roles (the honourable nobleman, the virtuous wife or the inspired artist) and the perception of lives in terms of certain plots (the rise from rags to riches, for instance, or the sinner's repentance or conversion).

An early example of this approach is William Tindall's *John Bunyan, Mechanick Preacher* (1934). Tindall treated Bunyan's *Grace Abounding to the Chief of Sinners* in the 1930s style, as a product typical in all but its literary skill of Bunyan's class, the artisans or 'mechanics'. However, Tindall also placed *Grace Abounding* in a particular literary genre, the 'enthusiastic autobiography' or conversion narrative that appeared in England in the middle of the seventeenth century and was associated with radical Protestant sects such as Baptists and Quakers.

Works in this genre followed the models of St Augustine's *Confessions* and the life of St Paul as told in the *Acts of the Apostles*, first stressing early sinfulness and then telling the story of a dramatic change of heart. Tindall discusses what he calls the 'conventions' of the genre, the 'patterns of selection, emphasis and arrangement', and 'the rigid formula of regeneration', noting that these how-to-write-it rules originated in an oral environment, the meeting.

In similar fashion, some scholarly biographies have focused on the self-presentation or self-fashioning of their subjects. This is what Stephen Greenblatt did in *Sir Walter Raleigh: The Renaissance Man and his Roles* (1973), followed by his more famous study of *Renaissance Self-Fashioning from More to Shakespeare* (1980). Felipe Fernandez-Armesto's *Columbus* (1991) differs from earlier biographies of the great discoverer by emphasizing the protagonist's lifelong concern with self-advancement and self-promotion. It describes Columbus as 'exhibitionistic' even in his show of humility and as playing a role that was 'uncannily well scripted'.

Again, a recent biography of William Butler Yeats by the Irish historian Roy Foster places considerable stress on the poet's self-presentation; his clothes, for instance (especially the black cloak and sombrero), his theatrical gestures, his way of speaking or rather intoning his poems in public, his concern with the frontispiece portraits in his books, his autobiographies, and finally what a contemporary described in 1915 as Yeats's concern with 'building up a legend around himself'. An earlier study by Richard Ellmann had already emphasized what the author called Yeats's 'poses' and his 'masks'.[14]

Historians have also been showing increasing interest in catching people in the act of trying on or constructing different identities for themselves, in 'passing' for what they were not – passing for white, for a man, for a member of the upper classes and so on. Some well-known cases of women who dressed as men and served in the army or navy before being discovered have taken on a new significance in the context of current concerns with identity and its plasticity as well as with the history of women.[15]

A minor figure who has become a focus of scholarly attention in this way is George Psalmanazar, a Frenchman who experimented with a number of careers before coming to England and attempting to pass himself off as a native of Formosa. He published a detailed description of the island in 1704 before he was unmasked as an impostor. As a recent study emphasizes, Psalmanazar 'played many parts . . . He was Japanese, Formosan, Frenchman, Dutchman, Jew, student, picaro, refugee, soldier, convert, polemicist, fraud, scholar, hack, entrepreneur, penitent, exemplar and elder.'[16]

Performances and Occasions

Psalmanazar may be viewed as a skilled performer, and the recent interest in his career is a symptom of what may be called a 'performative turn' in cultural history. The importance of the dramaturgical model in the 1950s and '60s has already been noted (see p. 36). However, from the 1970s onwards there has been a gradual, subtle, collective shift in the way in which this model has been used.

Performing cultural history

Historians, like their colleagues in other disciplines, have been shifting from the notion of a social 'script' to one of social 'performance', a term that was first brought into theoretical prominence in the 1970s by anthropologists working on gossip and ritual. A little later, another anthropologist, Marshall Sahlins, launched the more general idea of culture as a series of recipes for carrying out 'performatives', a term borrowed from the English philosopher John Austin, who had studied speech acts such as 'I name this ship' or – in the context of marriage – 'I will', utterances that do not so much describe situations as bring them about.[17]

The history of political ideas has been rewritten from this point of view, notably by Quentin Skinner in *Foundations of Modern Political Thought* (1978), concerned as he was with what the authors he discussed were doing in writing their books, the point of their arguments, what Austin called their 'illocutionary force'. By focusing on words as actions in a political, social and intellectual context, Skinner made a contribution to what he called 'a history of political theory with a genuinely historical character'.[18]

Another example, less well known outside France, is Christian Jouhaud's *Mazarinades* (1985), a study of the five thousand-odd pamphlets directed against the regime of cardinal Mazarin in the middle of the seventeenth century. Jouhaud rejected the statistical approach to these pamphlets practised by some of his predecessors (see p. 22), just as he rejected approaches to these *mazarinades* as passive 'reflections' of the public opinion of the time. The 'fluidity' of their discourse, as he calls it, makes it impossible to approach these slippery texts in a traditional manner. Instead, the author asks, like Austin and Skinner, 'what this writing *does*', and presents the pamphlets as so many actions, as texts needing discussion in terms of their strategies, their tactics, their staging (*mise-en-scène*), their reception and their efficacity.

Public festivals are more obviously amenable to analysis in terms of performance and they have indeed been analysed in this way, as in the case of Queen Elizabeth II's coronation, interpreted as a 'performance of consensus', or popular festivals in Venezuela viewed as performances of nationalism. Commemorations have been described as performances of history or memory. Dance history, once the province of specialists, is now taken seriously by cultural historians and discussed in relation to politics and society.[19]

The concept is also used in analyses of everyday life in terms of the performance of ethnicity, for instance, gender, honour, courtiership, nobility or slavery. Thus Michael Herzfeld's ethnography of a village in Crete presented the coffee-house as a stage for the performance of masculinity through ritualized aggression – card-games, for instance, in which 'almost every move is made with aggressive gestures, especially by the striking of the knuckles against the table as the card is flung down'.[20]

Displays of submission to masters by slaves have been interpreted as performances, as 'putting on', as exaggeration (see p. 39). Working-class deference has been interpreted in similar terms. Conversely, as the anthropologist James Scott puts it, 'If subordination requires a credible performance of humility and deference, so domination seems to require a credible performance of haughtiness and mastery.'[21]

Linguists too have been speaking of 'acts of identity' to emphasize the fact that language creates or helps to create identities as well as expressing them. There is a growing interest in the performance of metaphor. The sweeping of floors, for instance, may function as a symbol of inner order. Ethnic cleansing may be seen as an enactment of a metaphor of purity.[22]

The term 'performance' has even been applied to architecture, developing an older idea of buildings or squares as stages. In the time of Pope Alexander VII, who commissioned the construction of St Peter's Square in Rome, the square was described as a 'theatre'. Architecture is a collective art in which the plan may be viewed as a kind of script that allows room for improvisation on the part of the craftsmen.[23]

What is the significance of the rise of the concept of performance? It is important to note what is rejected. The notion of a fixed cultural rule goes out, replaced by the idea of improvisation. Pierre Bourdieu, one of the chief initiators of the change in approach – though he rarely if ever used the term 'performance' – introduced his concept of the 'habitus' (the principle of regulated improvisation), in reaction against the structuralist notion of culture as a system of rules, a notion he found to be too rigid.

Improvisation in the literal sense has been analysed at length in a series of studies of oral culture. One of the most important of these, still all-too-rarely discussed by cultural historians, is a book which I must confess made a great impression on me when it first appeared: Albert Lord's *The Singer of Tales* (1960).[24] Lord had accompanied Milman

Parry to Yugoslavia, as it then was, in the 1930s. Parry, a Harvard Professor of Classics, believed that the *Iliad* and the *Odyssey* were oral compositions that had been written down from recitation.

To test this hypothesis Parry and Lord went to Bosnia, where epic poets or singers were still active in taverns and coffee-houses. They tape-recorded and analysed hundreds of epics, noting that the same poet performed the 'same' story differently on different occasions, making it longer or shorter or adapting it in other ways. In short, the poets improvised.

Extemporization for hours at a time was possible thanks to a framework of what Parry and Lord called 'formulas' and 'themes'. Once again, we find a stress on cultural schemata, this time at two different levels. A formula is a recurrent phrase or couplet such as 'across the level plain' or, in Homer's case, 'wine-dark sea'. A theme is a formula writ large, a recurrent episode such as the sending of a letter or the arming of the hero, an episode with a basic structure allowing for elaboration or 'ornaments' according to the skill of the singer or the nature of the occasion at which he is performing.

Now that orality has joined literacy and numeracy as a proper topic of historical research, historians are rediscovering many formulas and themes of this kind, just as they are paying more attention than before to rumours, ballads and folktales.[25] All the same, the analysis presented in *The Singer of Tales* remains without peer.

In the 1980s, the idea of performance took on a wider meaning. Older studies of rituals and festivals often assumed that they followed texts closely, noting that printed accounts of festivals were often published in the sixteenth and seventeenth centuries, sometimes even before the event had taken place. The texts were generally illustrated and some scholars assumed that the iconography of festivals could be analysed in the way that Panofsky and others analysed the iconography of paintings.

Recent studies of festivals, on the other hand, emphasize that 'performance is never mere enactment' or expression, but has a more active role, since the meaning is created anew on each occasion. Scholars now tend to stress the multiplicity and the conflict of the meanings of a given festival, a religious feast in South America, for instance, with Catholic associations for some participants but traditional African religious associations for others.

Historians of medieval and early modern Europe have often discussed the processions that played such an important part in religious and secular festivals alike as representations or embodiments of the social structure of the community. When doing this, however, it is necessary to be aware that consensus on these matters was far from complete, and that people might come to blows on the most solemn occasions because they held incompatible views of their place in the community, each certain that he or she had the right to precedence over the other.

Hence the new emphasis on what went wrong, on divergences from the script. A study of executions by Thomas Laqueur, for instance, criticizing Foucault and others for their emphasis on what he calls 'judicial dramaturgy', concentrates on the reactions of the crowd and the 'unexpected turns' which produced 'a theatre of far greater fluidity'.[26]

Again, in Renaissance Rome, the survival of the diaries of a papal master of ceremonies, Paris de Grassis, allows us to glimpse what really happened in papal rituals as well as what should have happened. For example, Grassis had to deal with elderly cardinals who found it difficult to stand or kneel for very long at a time, let alone walk in procession. To make matters still more difficult, the pope at the time was Julius II. Julius suffered from gout, so that he could not always genuflect when the liturgy required it. He did not like dressing up, and might appear without a stole when etiquette prescribed one. In addition, he was impatient of protocol. On one occasion when the master of ceremonies told him what he should be doing next, 'the pope smiled and said that he wanted to do things simply and in his own way'.[27]

The rise of occasionalism

The studies of performance, or of life as performance, discussed in the previous section suggest that we have been witnessing a quiet revolution in the practice of scholars in the humanities in one domain or discipline after another. In christening this trend 'occasionalism', I propose to adapt to the needs of cultural historians a philosophical term that was originally used by Kant to refer to late Cartesians such as Malebranche.

As we have seen, the same ritual or story varies on different occasions, while the expression of deference takes place only as long as the master is looking. Generalizing from examples such as these, we may say that on different occasions (moments, locales) or in different situations, in the presence of different people the same person behaves differently.

What I am calling 'occasionalism', if not exactly a shift from social determinism to individual freedom, is at least a move away from the idea of fixed reactions, following rules, and towards the notion of flexible responses, according to the 'logic' or the 'definition of the situation', a phrase made famous by the Chicago sociologist William I. Thomas. The work on self-presentation by another Chicago sociologist, Erving Goffman (see p. 38), offers one of the most vivid illustrations of the trend. In the 1950s, this occasionalist approach ran counter to dominant forms of social and historical analysis. In the last few years, by contrast, one seems to encounter it everywhere, in the most varied contexts or domains.

In the case of language, for instance, historians are learning from the sociolinguists to study the occasions on which bilingual people switch from one language to another, while others practise 'diglossia', using a 'high' variety of language to discuss politics, for example, and a 'low' variety to talk about football.

Bilingualism is an example of a more general phenomenon that may be called 'biculturalism'. We tend to think of handwriting as the expression of the individual personality. However, in sixteenth-century France, for instance, the handwriting of the same person might well vary in style according to the occasion. Particular styles of handwriting – court hand, secretary hand, merchant hand and so on – were associated with particular functions such as keeping accounts or writing letters to friends. In early modern Hungary, examples have been found of an individual signing his name on one occasion and making a cross on another.

Art historians too have been coming to think of style in relation to occasions as well as periods or individuals. Students of the Renaissance, for instance, have noted shifts from Gothic to classical – and back again – in the work of painters and sculptors such as Pisanello or Veit Stoss, according to the demands of either the genre or the patron.[28]

A similar point might be made about the civilizing process, presented in the classic study of 1939 by Norbert Elias (see pp. 10–11). In the case of the history of humour, for instance, the problem with the Elias thesis is that although the upper classes ceased to laugh at certain kinds of joke in public or in mixed company in the course of the seventeenth and eighteenth centuries, they appear to have continued laughing at these jokes in other locales. Members of the upper classes, ladies in particular, seem to have felt that their high social status required them not to show amusement at 'low' jokes whenever people from other groups could see and hear them. In the smoking-room, on the other hand, away from the ladies, Victorian gentlemen continued to appreciate these jokes. The ladies may have done the same in the absence of men.

Deconstruction

What now appears to some scholars to have been the naive realism of earlier generations of historians should not be exaggerated. Some of them were perfectly conscious of the active role of historians in constructing social categories. It was Frederick William Maitland, for instance, who remarked in the 1880s that 'were an examiner to ask who introduced the feudal system into England, one very good answer, if properly explained, would be Henry Spelman' (a seventeenth-century scholar interested in the history of medieval law).[29]

Again, the French historian Lucien Febvre wrote that 'our fathers fabricated their Renaissance', just as 'every age mentally fabricates its representation of the historical past' (*chaque époque se fabrique mentalement sa représentation du passé historique*).[30] In similar fashion, historians have been using the phrase 'the myth of the Renaissance' to register their awareness that the term is not so much an objective description as the projection of values on to the past.

Other scholars were well aware of the relation between history and myth. Francis Cornford's *Thucydides Mythistoricus* (1907), an analysis of 'myth' in the history written by Thucydides and the analogies between his work and Greek tragedy, appeared nearly seventy years before Hayden White's *Metahistory* (1973; see above, pp. 79–80) and other studies in what is sometimes described as 'mythistory'.

Again, nations have not always been considered as immutable. The first sentence of Americo Castro's famous *Structure of Spanish History* (1948) reads as follows: 'a country is not a fixed entity'. As the author goes on to explain, 'Spain, like any other nation, has been a problematic "subject" that has had to invent itself and maintain itself in the course of its existence.' The Mexican historian Edmundo O'Gorman's book *The Invention of America* was published in 1958. At the time, his argument that the discovery was less important than the idea of a fourth continent sounded odd, but it seems almost commonplace now.

However, the idea of construction is taken considerably further today. In his study of identity in Africa, *Mestizo Logic* (1990), the French anthropologist Jean-Loup Amselle argues that the Fulani or the Bambara should be regarded not as tribes or even as ethnic groups but as parts of a 'system of transformations'. His point is that there are no sharp cultural boundaries between these groups, while individuals have fluid or multiple identities, distinguishing themselves from different 'others' according to the circumstances. Identity is continually being reconstructed or negotiated.

The constructivist reaction against a simplified view of cultures or social groups as homogeneous and clearly divided from the outside world is a salutary one. The criticism of 'essentialism' by Amselle and others might usefully be applied not only to cultures such as the Fulani or to classes such as the bourgeoisie, but also to movements or periods such as the Renaissance or the Reformation, Romanticism or Impressionism. All the same, the idea of cultural construction raises problems that are still far from having been resolved, three problems in particular: who is doing the construction? under what constraints? out of what?

'Who invented Ireland?' asked Declan Kiberd at the beginning of his book *Inventing Ireland* (1996), noting that the Irish exiled abroad made a disproportionate contribution to the idea of an Irish nation and that the English also 'helped' in the work of construction. In the case of 'the Orient', the role of the West in constructing it as an opposite has become obvious enough, but the problem of the relative importance of different kinds of westerner – the traveller, the scholar, the missionary, the bureaucrat and so on – remains open. So does the question of the relative importance of individual and collective invention, and of the ways in which collective creativity works, by creative reception for instance.

A second problem concerns the possible cultural or social constraints on the process of construction. It is surely not the case that everything is imaginable at any time, that (say) a group of Spanish Americans were free to invent any kind of Argentina they wanted following their independence from Spain. The idea of cultural construction developed as part of a healthy reaction against economic and social determinism, but it is necessary to avoid over-reaction. Historians need to explore the limits to cultural plasticity, limits that are sometimes set by economic factors, sometimes by political ones, and sometimes by cultural traditions, even though they are capable of modification – up to a point.

A third problem concerns the materials of cultural construction. It would surely be a mistake to see it as a process of creation *ex nihilo*. In fact, Eric Hobsbawm already noted 'the use of ancient materials' in his introduction to *The Invention of Tradition*. Going a little further in this direction, and borrowing a term from the cosmologists, I should like to suggest that what was traditionally described as the transmission of a tradition (or, as Bourdieu called it, 'cultural reproduction') is more of a process of 'continuous creation'. Whatever the would-be transmitters think they are doing, the process of passing a culture on to a new generation is necessarily one of reconstruction, of what Lévi-Strauss called *bricolage* and Certeau, 're-employment' (see p. 77).

The process is driven in part by the need to adapt old ideas to new circumstances, in part by tensions between traditional forms and new messages, in part by what has been called 'the inner conflict of tradition', the conflict between the attempt to find universal solutions for human problems and the necessities or the logic of the situation. In the case of religious or political movements, the inevitable differences between founders and followers lead to cultural polarities. The message of the founder is often ambiguous. Indeed, some would say that founders succeed precisely because they signify many things to many people. When the followers try to interpret the founder's message, the latent contradictions become manifest.[31]

To investigate this process in greater depth is a task for the future. The problem of the future of cultural history will be addressed in the following chapter.

6
Beyond the Cultural Turn?

The phrase 'NCH' seemed a good idea when it was coined in the late 1980s, just as the 'New History' in the USA did in the 1910s. Unfortunately, novelty is a fast-diminishing cultural asset. This 'new' cultural history is over twenty years old. Indeed, an inspection of the chronological list of publications at the end of this volume suggests that it is already over thirty years old, since the real breakthrough occurred in the early 1970s, a decade before the invention of the slogan. The same list suggests that while the production of innovative work remained high in the 1980s – look at the range and the quality of the books first published in 1988, for example – it gradually declined in the 1990s. The early twenty-first century appears to be a moment of recognition, taking stock and consolidation, in which the present study has its place. It has to be said, however, that this kind of stock-taking generally follows the most creative phase of a cultural movement.

Add to this the fact that the NCH has been the object of serious criticisms, and it becomes impossible to avoid the question whether the time has come for a still newer phase, or whether this phase has already begun. We might also ask whether what comes next will be a still more radical movement or whether, on the contrary, we shall see a rapprochement with more traditional forms of history.

As usual, distinctions are in order. We have to distinguish what we want to happen from what we expect to happen, as well as separating short-term trends from long-term ones. So far as prediction is concerned, it is difficult to do more than extrapolate long-term trends, even if we are aware from past experience that the future will be more than a simple continuation of such trends. We have to allow for possible reactions against these trends, attempts to return to the past, although we know that a simple return to the past is impossible.

The most useful thing to do at this point is probably to discuss alternative scenarios. One possibility might be described as 'Burckhardt's return', using Burckhardt's name as a kind of shorthand, a symbol for the revival of traditional cultural history. A second possibility is the continuing expansion of the new cultural history into even more domains. A third possibility is a reaction against the constructivist reduction of society to culture, what might be called 'the revenge of social history'.

Burckhardt's Return

In a sense we cannot speak of Burckhardt's return because the old man never left town in the first place. That is, the history of high culture, that of the Renaissance, for example, or the Enlightenment, was never abandoned in the age of enthusiasm for popular culture in the 1970s and '80s, even if it suffered in the competition for academic resources.

Anthony Grafton makes a well-known example of a cultural historian whose scholarly work has focused on the history of the classical tradition in the Renaissance and beyond, although he has also contributed to the history of reading and produced a history of the footnote and its relation to the technical practices and the ideology of the historical profession in *The Footnote* (1997).

One of the best-known works of cultural history published in English in this period was Carl Schorske's *Fin-de-Siècle Vienna* (1979), a study of writers such as Arthur Schnitzler and Hugo von Hoffmannsthal, artists such as Gustav Klimt and Oskar Kokoschka, of Sigmund Freud and of Arnold Schoenberg. Schorske presented his work as a study of modernity, as defined against the historicism of the nineteenth century. His history of what he calls an 'a-historical culture' offers an essentially political interpretation of this movement, linking it to 'tremors of social and political disintegration' and to the decline of liberalism in the sense of a commitment to rationality, realism and progress. These were the values against which his protagonists rebelled in their different ways – Freud by stressing the irrational forces of the psyche, for instance, Klimt by breaking with realism and deliberately offending bourgeois morality, and so on.

One possible future for cultural history – in the near future at least – is that of a revival of emphasis on the history of high culture. High culture is, after all, a conspicuous absence from 'Cultural Studies' as it is studied and taught in many places today. If this revival or return were to take place, it is unlikely that the history of popular culture would wither away, even though the concept 'popular culture' has been called into question. The two kinds of cultural history would probably co-exist, together with increasing interest in the interactions between them. Indeed, high culture might be reframed or even decentred, stressing (say) the reception of the Enlightenment by different social groups or the domestication of the Renaissance in the sense of its impact on everyday life, on the design of chairs and plates, for instance, as well as paintings and palaces, on the history of mentalities as well as the history of philosophy. Indeed, this shift in emphasis is already taking place.[1]

Some leading examples of the NCH might be reread from this point of view, Ginzburg's *Cheese and Worms* (1976) for example. This vivid portrait of an individual and his cosmos has appealed to many people without a special interest in sixteenth-century Italy. It can also be read, however, as a contribution to the history of a major cultural movement, the Counter-Reformation, from the angle of its reception, its interaction with traditional popular culture. In short, as so often happens in cultural history, an attempted return to the past will produce something new. Some recent attempts to revive – but also to redefine – the idea of tradition, point in the same direction.

Politics, Violence and Emotions

A second scenario predicts the extension of the new cultural history to include domains previously neglected, among them politics, violence and the emotions.

The cultural history of politics

Politics and culture are linked in more than one way. One set of possible connections was explored by Schorske in *Fin-de-Siècle Vienna*. Another approach might be described as a politics of culture, ranging from the publicity given to the collecting activities of rulers as signs of their magnificence and good taste to national or nationalist reasons for the foundation of galleries, museums and theatres in the nineteenth century.

A concern with what is sometimes called 'cultural management' is particularly visible in the nineteenth and twentieth centuries. In Brazil, for instance, it was the regime of President Vargas, especially between 1930 and 1945, that particularly concerned itself with national culture, although, as a recent study suggests, this was also a time of 'culture wars' in the sense of competition between ministries, for instance, or between architectural styles in the name of representing the identity of the nation.[2]

However, it is the culture of politics that most deserves attention here. It would be misleading to suggest that cultural historians have always ignored politics, or that political historians have totally neglected culture. There was a place for politics in traditional cultural history, including the work of Burckhardt on the Renaissance state as a work of art, of Marc Bloch on the healing powers attributed to the rulers of France and England, and of many scholars on the symbolism of monarchy – regalia, coronations, funerals or formal entries into cities.

In political studies, some leading figures, such as Murray Edelman, author of *Politics as Symbolic Action* (1971), made their 'cultural turn' a generation ago, examining political rituals or quasi-rituals and other symbolic aspects of political behaviour in the present and in the past. The cultural explanation offered by F. S. L. Lyons for the troubled political history of Ireland was discussed in an earlier chapter (see p. 33).

All the same, when new technical terms come into use, this is usually a sign of a shift in interests or approaches. The concept of 'political culture' is an expression of the need to link the two domains, focusing on the political attitudes or assumptions of different groups of people, and the ways in which these attitudes are instilled. Employed by political scientists in the 1960s, the phrase seems to have entered the discourse of historians in the late 1980s, to judge by the titles of books such as Keith Baker's *The Political Culture of the Old Regime* (1987), whether the phrase was used about a whole country or about a group, such as women.

The study of the French Revolution by Lynn Hunt, a leading figure in the NCH, was centrally concerned with political culture. *Politics, Culture and Class in the French Revolution* (1984) focused on changes in 'the rules of political behaviour' and more especially new 'symbolic practices', studied in the manner of Foucault. These practices ranged from the choreography of public festivals to wearing a tricolour cockade or the red cap of liberty, or addressing everyone by the familiar 'tu' or 'citoyen(ne)' in order to symbolize equality and fraternity and to contribute by small gestures to the realization of those ideals. A book that began as a social history of politics, so the author confesses, was transformed into cultural history, though the careful distinction between the ways in which women and men, for example, participated in this new political culture betrays the former social historian.

Another recent example of the interweaving of political and cultural history comes from the collective work of the Subaltern Studies Group, based in India and led by Ranajit Guha. The group's project, which has led to an extended debate, has been nothing less than to rewrite Indian history, especially the history of the movement for Indian independence before 1947. The aim was to give their due place to different dominated groups (the 'subaltern classes', as Gramsci used to call them) alongside the elites whose activities filled earlier histories of independence. In this respect, the work of Edward Thompson – whose father worked in India and sympathized with the independence movement – has been an inspiration.[3]

The work published by the Subaltern Studies Group has also been distinctive in its concern with political culture, especially with the culture informing 'the subaltern condition'. Works of literature as well as official documents have been employed as sources for 'the mentality of subalternity'. Here too Edward Thompson has been a model, although, unlike Thompson, the group has always taken a strong interest in cultural theory, including the work of Lévi-Strauss, Foucault and Derrida.

For a concrete example of the group's approach, one might turn to Shahid Amin's study of the image of Gandhi in 'peasant consciousness', which emphasizes the way in which 'pre-existing patterns of popular belief' shaped this image (yet again, we see the interest in schemata). Stories circulated describing Gandhi's occult powers, while the cult of the leader was a secular version of the devotion (*bhakti*) to Krishna and other gods. This study illuminates some of the questions about the transmission of tradition raised in chapter 5. On one side, we may say that religious traditions were being secularized. On the other, it is clear that political attitudes and practices were deeply influenced by religious beliefs. 'Cultural hybridization' rather than 'the modernization of tradition' would seem to be the best description of the process analysed by Amin.[4]

Aided by the rise of international interest in postcolonial studies, the movement has attracted increasing attention outside India. A Latin American Subaltern Studies group has been founded, while an article written in 1996 examines the influence of the 'subaltern approach' on histories of Ireland.[5] The reception of the work of the Subaltern Studies group makes a good example of the globalization of historical writing today as well as illustrating the links between culture and politics in the present no less than in the past. It also illustrates how ideas are tested in the process of attempting to employ them outside the context for which they were originally developed.

Despite these studies of political culture, a number of important themes are still waiting for their cultural historians. The links between politics and the media are only just beginning to be explored, with studies of 'news culture' such as the role of news-books in the English civil war or the politics of court scandal.[6] The opportunities are particularly obvious in the case of the nineteenth and twentieth centuries, since the NCH has been dominated by specialists on the Middle Ages and the early modern period. No one, as far as I know, has yet attempted to write the historical anthropology of parliaments, or the modern diplomatic corps and its rituals, although studies have been made of festivals in the age of nationalism.[7]

The cultural history of violence

If there is no historical anthropology of the modern army, there is at least a study of the First World War from the perspective of the history of the body. The military historian John Keegan, well known for his social history of battles, now argues that war is a cultural phenomenon. A recent volume of essays on a traditional theme in political and military history, the Thirty Years War, treats it from the perspective of the everyday life of ordinary people.[8] The First World War in particular has been discussed from the cultural point of view, focusing on the threat of war in shaping the generation of 1914, for instance, or on the cultural effects of the war, including the relation between war and modernity.[9]

Historians of castles are turning towards culture, rejecting military determinism – in other words, an explanation of castle building purely in terms of defence – and emphasizing instead the importance of displaying wealth, power and hospitality – in other words, the castle as theatre. Even naval history is beginning to be approached from this point of view, for example in a recent study of the North Sea as a 'maritime theatre' for naval spectacles mounted by Britain and Germany around 1900, the cultural aspect of their arms race.[10]

It is all too easy to see why the topic of violence is currently attracting cultural historians more than ever before. The suggestion that violence has a cultural history may sound surprising, since it is often seen as the eruption of a volcano, the expression of human drives that have nothing to do with culture. The argument that violence is a kind of drama may even seem scandalous, since it is real blood that is shed. However, the point of the drama analogy is not to deny the bloodshed. The Dutch anthropologist Anton Blok put his finger on the key problem when he noted the importance of reading the messages sent by the violent, the symbolic elements in their action (even if the agents themselves may not be conscious of the symbolism). The point of the cultural approach is to reveal the meaning of apparently 'meaningless' violence, the rules that govern its employment. As Keith Baker has remarked: 'The action of a rioter in picking up a stone can no more be understood apart from the symbolic field that gives it meaning than the action of a priest in picking up a sacramental vessel.' Thus a lynching in the nineteenth-century American South has been studied as 'a moral scenario' and the riots in Naples in 1647 as a 'social drama', by historians who drew on the work of the anthropologists Mary Douglas and Victor Turner.[11]

The violence of crowds in the French religious wars of the later sixteenth century has attracted particular attention from historians. The pioneer, here as elsewhere, was Natalie Davis. It was thinking about the Holocaust and the political violence of the 1960s that encouraged her to see the sixteenth century in a new light. A similar approach has also been followed by several French historians, notably Denis Crouzet.[12]

These historians differ among themselves on many points, but they also have a good deal in common, Davis and Crouzet in particular. They note the important role of young men and even boys in the acts of violence, whether this is to be explained by festive licence or by the traditional association of children with innocence. They reconstruct the cultural repertory of actions available to the participants, a repertory taken in part from the liturgy, in part from the rituals of the law and in part from the mystery plays of the time. They discuss the ludic or carnivalesque aspects of the riots, drawing on the ideas of Mikhail Bakhtin on festive violence.

They also consider the religious meanings of the events. Crouzet compares the rioters to people who are 'possessed' by gods or spirits in the course of religious rituals. Davis suggests that we should read the riots as rituals of purification, attempts to rid the community of pollution. Drawing on the discussion of performance in chapter 5, we might say that the rioters enacted the metaphor of purification. We may also suggest that their actions helped construct their community by dramatizing the exclusion of outsiders.[13]

We may reasonably expect future studies of ethnic cleansing and of what might be called the 'cultural history of terrorism'.[14]

The cultural history of emotions

The violence discussed in the previous section was the expression of strong emotions. Do the emotions have a history? Nietzsche thought so. He complained in *The Gay Science* (1882) that 'so far, everything that has given colour to existence still lacks a history . . . where could one find a history of love, of avarice, of envy, of conscience, of piety, or of cruelty?'

Some of the historians discussed in earlier chapters would have agreed, beginning with Jacob Burckhardt, whose references to envy, anger and love in Renaissance Italy Nietzsche somehow overlooked, despite his personal acquaintance with the author.[15] In his *Autumn of the Middle Ages*, Johan Huizinga discussed what he called 'the passionate and violent soul of the age', the emotional oscillation and the lack of self-control characteristic of individuals in that period. Twenty years later, Norbert Elias used Huizinga's study as a base for his own cultural history of the emotions, more especially of attempts to control the emotions as part of the 'civilizing process' (see p. 53).

Despite these examples, it is only relatively recently that the majority of historians have taken emotions seriously. A history of tears, for example, would have been almost inconceivable before the 1980s, at least outside certain circles in France, but today tears are seen as part of history, more especially the history of the 'affective revolution' of the late eighteenth century, the context for the weeping readers of Rousseau.[16]

In the English-speaking world, an interest in the history of the emotions is particularly associated with Peter Gay,

Theodore Zeldin and with Peter and Carol Stearns. Zeldin turned from the politics of Napoleon III to what he calls (following the Goncourt brothers), the 'intimate history' of ambition, love, worry and other emotions in nineteenth-century France, while Peter Gay, following a training in psychoanalysis, moved from the intellectual history of the Age of Reason to the psychohistory of the loves and hates of the nineteenth-century bourgeoisie.[17]

As for Carol and Peter Stearns, between them they have published a manifesto for historical 'emotionology', monographs on anger and jealousy, and a more general study of changes in emotional 'style' in the USA in the early twentieth century (*American Cool* (1994)). They argue the case for three kinds of change; in the emphasis given to emotions in general; in the relative importance of specific feelings; and in the control or 'management' of emotions.

An alternative framework has recently been proposed by William Reddy in *The Navigation of Feeling* (2001). Drawing on both the anthropology and the psychology of the emotions, Reddy presents a cluster of connected concepts. Like Carol and Peter Stearns, he emphasizes emotional 'management' or, as he calls it, 'navigation', at both an individual and a social level. Linked to this notion is his idea of an 'emotional regime'. However, his approach also exemplifies the recent 'performative turn' (see p. 90). Reddy discusses the language of emotions in terms of 'performative utterances'. A declaration of love, for instance, is not, or not only, an expression of feelings. It is a strategy to encourage, amplify or even transform the feelings of the beloved.

Standing back from these suggestions, the implications of which have still to be worked out, it may be suggested that historians of the emotions face a basic dilemma. They have to decide whether they are maximalists or minimalists, in other words whether they believe in the essential historicity or non-historicity of emotions. Either it is the case that specific emotions, or the whole package of emotions in a given culture (the local 'culture of emotions', as Stearns and Stearns call it), are subject to fundamental changes over time; or that they remain essentially the same in different periods.

Scholars who choose the 'minimalist' horn of the dilemma are forced to limit themselves to the study of conscious attitudes to the emotions. They write sound intellectual history, but it is not really the history of the emotions themselves. On the other side, the scholars who choose the 'maximalist' option are more innovative. The price they pay is that their conclusions are much more difficult to support. Evidence of conscious attitudes to anger, fear, love and so on are not difficult to unearth from surviving documents, but conclusions about fundamental changes over the long term are necessarily much more speculative.

In a well-known study, the classicist Eric Dodds, borrowing a phrase from his friend the poet W. H. Auden, described the late classical period as an 'age of anxiety'. *Pagan and Christian in an Age of Anxiety* (1965) is a book full of insights, focusing on religious experience but also discussing dreams and attitudes to the body. However, the title of the book raises a problem which the author does little to resolve. Are people more anxious in one historical period than in another, rather than suffering from different anxieties? Even if this were the case, how could a historian possibly find evidence to establish it?

The cultural history of perception

The increasing interest in the history of senses runs parallel to the interest in the emotions. There is a tradition of studies of sight (for example Smith's *European Vision and the South Pacific* (1959) and Baxandall's *Painting and Experience in Fifteenth-Century Italy* (1972)), as well as the work on the gaze inspired by Foucault. Occasional references to the sound of the past were made by Johan Huizinga and Gilberto Freyre, who described the swish of skirts on the stairs of the Great House in colonial Brazil. It was, once again, Freyre who described nineteenth-century Brazilian bedrooms as smelling of a combination of feet, damp, urine and semen. Today, however, we find ambitious attempts to write about all the senses in some detail.

In *Rembrandt's Eyes* (1999), for instance, Simon Schama tries with characteristic boldness to present the city of Amsterdam in the seventeenth century as it presented itself to all five senses. He evokes the smells of the city, especially salt, rotting wood and night-soil, and in certain places herbs and spices. He describes the sounds of the city, the chiming of many clocks, 'the slap of canal water against the bridges', the sawing of wood and, in what he calls 'the clanging zone', where weapons were made, the sound of hammering on metal. Readers may be wondering what the sources for such an evocative account might be, so it is worth noting the value of travelogues in this respect, since travellers are hypersensitive to sensations to which they are unaccustomed.

Smell and sound are the domains on which most has been written in the last few years, notably by the French historian Alain Corbin. In *The Foul and the Fragrant* (1986), a study in what the author calls 'the French social imagination', Corbin stresses modes of perception, sensibilities, the symbolism of smells and hygienic practices. In a creative adaptation of an idea from Norbert Elias, Corbin links these practices to a lowering of the 'threshold' of tolerance for bad smells at the beginning of the nineteenth century, a time of bourgeois revulsion to what was perceived as the 'stench of the poor'. As another scholar puts it, 'smell is cultural' in the sense that 'odours are invested with cultural values', just as smell is historical, because its associations change over time.

In the wake of Corbin, and of novels such as Patrick Süskind's *Perfume* (1985), set in eighteenth-century France and telling the story of a man obsessed with smell, the subject is attracting more historians. So far they have concentrated on the gulf between the – more or less – de-odorized 'smell culture' of the twentieth century and that of earlier epochs. As research progresses, it is to be hoped that other major distinctions will emerge.[18]

From smell, Corbin turned to the history of sound in his *Village Bells* (1994), concerned with what he calls the history of the 'soundscape' (*le paysage sonore*) and 'the culture of the senses' (*culture sensible*). It was appropriate that a French historian should have opened up this domain, since Lucien Febvre suggested in the 1940s that the sixteenth century was the age of the ear. The debate on the primacy of different senses in different periods now seems rather sterile, but Corbin shows that the history of sound can be written in another way. For example, he makes the point that bells were heard differently in the past because they were associated with piety or parochialism – in French, *l'esprit de clocher*. As these associations became weaker, the threshold of tolerance was raised and people began to express objections to the invasion of their ears by the sound of bells. As in the case of smell, Corbin was a little ahead of his time, but there is now a significant cluster of historical studies of sound.[19]

Most histories of sound concentrate on what they call 'noise', but the history of music can also be approached from this direction as a form of the history of perception. In *Listening in Paris* (1995), James Johnson offers a cultural history of the perception of music in the eighteenth and nineteenth centuries, drawing, paradoxical as it may seem, on the evidence of images as well as texts, and arguing for the rise of a 'new way of listening' at the end of the Old Regime. The revolution in listening, according to Johnson, consisted in the first place of attending to the music rather than whispering or looking at other members of the audience, in the second place of increasingly emotional engagement with the sound rather than the words – at this point the book exemplifies the turn to the history of reception discussed earlier (see pp. 60, 78). Like the readers of the time, especially the readers of Rousseau, Paris audiences of the late eighteenth century wept floods of tears at the opera or the concert hall. The moral of this example is the importance of writing a general history of the senses rather than one that is split into seeing, hearing, smelling and so on.

The Revenge of Social History

An alternative scenario to the expansion of the NCH is that of a reaction against it, an increasingly acute sense that its empire has become over-extended, that too much political or social territory has been lost to 'culture'. The idea of a shift 'from the social history of culture to the cultural history of society' (see p. 74) does not please everyone. The idea of cultural construction is sometimes interpreted as an example of 'subjectivist epistemology', a retreat from verification, a belief that 'anything goes'.[20]

The reaction against the NCH or at least against certain aspects of it, or claims made for it, might be explained in terms of the pendulum swings that so often occur in history, or by the need of a new generation of scholars to define themselves against an older group and to take their place in the sun.

All the same, it is only honest to admit that the reaction also stems from weaknesses in the NCH programme, problems that time – together with certain critics – has gradually exposed. Besides the limits of constructivism, discussed in the previous chapter, three problems are particularly serious: the definition of culture, the methods to be followed in the NCH and the danger of fragmentation.

Once too exclusive, the definition of culture has become too inclusive (see p. 29). Particularly problematic today is the relation between social and cultural history. The phrase 'socio-cultural history' has become common currency. In Britain, the Social History Society has recently redefined its interests to include culture. Whether we describe what is happening as social history swallowing cultural history or as the reverse, we are witnessing the emergence of a hybrid genre. The genre can be practised in different fashions, with some historians placing more emphasis on the cultural half and others on the social. Historians of reading, for instance, may focus on specific texts, without forgetting the variety of their readers, or they may concentrate on different groups of reader, without excluding the content of what was read.

At the moment, the terms 'social' and 'cultural' seem to be used almost interchangeably to describe the history of dreams, for example, of language, of humour, of memory or of time. Distinctions might be useful. My own inclination would be to reserve the term 'cultural' for the history of phenomena that seem 'natural', such as dreams, memory and time. On the other hand, since language and humour are obviously cultural artefacts, it seems more appropriate to employ the term 'social' to refer to a particular approach to their history.

However we use the two terms, the relation between 'culture' and 'society' remains problematic. A generation ago, in his essay 'Thick Description' (see above, p. 36), one of the main instigators of the cultural turn, Clifford Geertz, had already noted the danger that cultural analysis 'will lose touch with the hard surfaces of life' such as economic and political structures. He was surely right in his prediction, and it is to be hoped that in what we might call a 'post-postmodern age', connections will be re-established.

However valuable the constructivist project for the 'cultural history of society' may be, it is no substitute for the social history of culture, including the history of constructivism itself. It may well be time to go beyond the cultural turn. As Victoria Bonnell and Lynn Hunt have suggested, the idea of the social should not be jettisoned but reconfigured.[21] Historians of reading, for instance, need to study 'communities of interpretation', historians of religion, 'communities of belief', historians of practice, 'communities of practice', historians of language, 'speech communities', and so on. In fact, the studies of the reception of texts and images discussed earlier (see pp. 60, 78) normally ask the great social question, 'Who?'. In other words, what kinds of people were looking at these objects in a particular place and time?

Controversies over definition are linked to controversies over method. Like the French *nouvelle histoire* of the 1970s, the NCH extended the territory of the historian, finding new objects of study such as smell and noise, reading and collecting, spaces and bodies. Traditional sources were not sufficient for the purpose, and relatively new kinds of source, from fiction to images, were pressed into service. New sources, however, require their own forms of source criticism, and the rules for reading pictures as historical evidence, to take just one example, are still unclear.[22]

Again, the idea that culture is a text that anthropologists or historians may read is an enticing one, but it is also deeply problematic. In any case, it is worth noting that historians and anthropologists do not use the metaphor of reading in the same way. As Roger Chartier has pointed out, Geertz studied the cockfight in Bali by observing specific fights and speaking to the participants, while Darnton analysed his cat massacre on the basis of an eighteenth-century text describing the incident (see chapter 3).

A fundamental problem with the metaphor of reading is that it seems to license intuition. Who is in a position to arbitrate when two intuitive readers disagree? Is it possible to formulate rules of reading, or at least to identify misreadings?

In the case of rituals, the debate is only just beginning. A recent critique has attempted to eliminate the concept from the vocabulary of historians of the early Middle Ages, arguing for a lack of fit between anthropological models and the texts surviving from the ninth or tenth centuries. The warning is well taken in the sense that if we are going to describe certain events as 'rituals', we need to be clear about the criteria for doing so. If, on the other hand, we think, as suggested above, in terms of more or less ritualized practices, the problem dissolves.[23]

In any case, to think of pursuing the subject by one method alone impoverishes cultural history. Different problems require different methods of response. Abandoned by a number of scholars in the course of the cultural turn, quantitative methods turn out to have their uses in cultural no less than in traditional social history. In the work of the French historian Daniel Roche, for instance, whether he is studying the history of academies, the history of books or the history of clothes (see p. 68), a happy blend of quantitative and qualitative methods can be found.

In the third place, there is the problem of fragmentation. As we saw in chapter 1, the early cultural historians had holist ambitions. They liked to make connections. More recently, some distinguished cultural historians, in the United States in particular, have advocated the cultural approach as a remedy for fragmentation, 'a possible basis for the reintegration of American historiography'.[24]

The problem is that culture often seems to act as a force encouraging fragmentation, whether in the United States, in Ireland or in the Balkans. The contribution of cultural differences to political conflicts in Ireland has already been discussed (see p. 33). A similar argument about *The Disuniting of America* (1992) has been put forward by another historian, Arthur M. Schlesinger Junior, emphasizing what is lost by the current prominence of ethnic identities in the United States.

At a very different level the rise of the intellectual trend described above as 'occasionalism' (see chapter 5) implies a fragmented view of social groups or even the individual self. It is a characteristically 'postmodern' view in the sense of viewing the world as a more fluid, flexible, unpredictable place than it used to seem in the 1950s or '60s, whether to sociologists, social anthropologists or social historians. The rise of micro-history is surely part of this trend, even if Natalie Davis, say, Emmanuel Le Roy Ladurie or Carlo Ginzburg vehemently deny any postmodernist intentions.[25]

Like ethnographers, micro-historians face the problem of the relation between the small groups they study in detail and larger wholes. As Geertz himself stated the problem in 'Thick Description', it is 'how to get from a collection of ethnographic miniatures . . . to wall-sized culturescapes of the nation, the epoch, the continent or the civilization'. His study of the cockfight often speaks about 'the Balinese', but a reader may be permitted to wonder whether the attitudes discussed are shared by everyone in Bali or by men alone or by men from certain social groups, possibly excluding the elite.

In similar fashion, as we have seen, some criticisms of Darnton's 'cat massacre' focused on the question whether it is permissible for a historian to draw conclusions about national characteristics from a single small incident. The study raises Geertz's question in a still more acute form, since the anthropologist used a study of a village to reach conclusions about a small island, while the historian had to bridge the gap between a group of apprentices and the population of eighteenth-century France. For whom, one might ask, was the cat massacre funny?

In short, cultural historians have not run short of problems. In what follows I shall discuss some recent work on frontiers, encounters and narrative to see if any of it offers solutions to at least some of the difficulties raised above.

Frontiers and Encounters

In 1949, Fernand Braudel was already discussing in his famous book, *Mediterranean*, the importance of 'cultural frontiers' such as the Rhine and the Danube, from ancient Rome to the Reformation. Yet it is only relatively recently that the term has come into frequent use in different languages, perhaps because it offers cultural historians a way of countering fragmentation.

The idea of a cultural frontier is an attractive one. One might even say that it is too attractive, because it encourages users to slip without noticing from the literal to the metaphorical uses of the term, failing to distinguish between geographical frontiers and those between social classes, for instance, between sacred and profane, serious and comic, history and fiction. What follows will concentrate on the borders between cultures.

Here too, distinctions are in order, between the views from outside and from inside a given culture, for instance. From outside, frontiers often appear to be objective and even mappable. Students of the history of literacy in France, between the seventeenth and the nineteenth centuries in particular, are familiar with the famous diagonal line from St Malo to Geneva, distinguishing a north-eastern zone of higher literacy from a south-western zone where fewer people were able to read. Other cultural maps show the distribution of monasteries or universities or presses in different parts of Europe, or the distribution of adherents to different religions in India.

Maps of this kind are an effective form of communication that is often more rapid and more memorable than a paraphrase in words. All the same, like words and figures, maps can mislead. They seem to imply homogeneity within a given 'culture area' and a sharp distinction between such areas. The continuum between German and Dutch (say) has to be turned into a sharp line, while small groups of Hindus in a predominantly Muslim area become invisible.

The view from outside needs to be supplemented by one from inside, stressing the experience of crossing the boundaries between 'us' and 'them' and encountering Otherness with a capital O (or perhaps with a capital A, since the French were the first to produce a theory of *l'Autre*). We are dealing here with the symbolic boundaries of imagined communities, boundaries that resist mapping. All the same, historians cannot afford to forget their existence.

Another useful distinction concerns the functions of cultural frontiers. Historians and geographers used to view them primarily as barriers. Today, on the other hand, the emphasis tends to fall on frontiers as meeting-places or 'contact zones'. Both conceptions have their uses.[26]

Walls and barbed wire cannot keep out ideas, but it does not follow that cultural barriers do not exist. There are at least some physical, political or cultural obstacles, including language and religion, which slow down cultural movements or divert them into different channels. Braudel was particularly interested in zones of resistance to cultural trends, in 'refusal to borrow', as he called it, associating this refusal with the resilience of civilizations, their power of survival. His examples included the long Japanese resistance to the chair and the table and the 'rejection' of the Reformation in the Mediterranean world.[27]

Another famous example of rejection is the resistance to print in the Islamic world, a resistance that lasted until the end of the eighteenth century. Indeed, the world of Islam has been viewed as a barrier separating the two zones in which books were printed, East Asia and Europe. The so-called 'gunpowder empires' (Ottoman, Persian and Mughal) were not hostile to innovation in technology, but they remained manuscript empires or 'calligraphic states' until the year 1800 of thereabouts.

An incident that occurred in Istanbul in the early eighteenth century revealed the strength of these forces of resistance. A Hungarian convert to Islam (formerly a Protestant clergyman) sent a memorandum to the sultan arguing for the importance of the press, and in 1726 he was given official permission to print secular books. However, there was opposition to this enterprise from religious leaders. The press printed only a handful of books and it did not last for very long. It was only in the nineteenth century that Islam and print negotiated an alliance.[28]

The second function of a cultural frontier is the opposite of the first: a meeting-place or contact zone. Borders are not infrequently regions with a distinctively hybrid culture of their own. In the early modern Balkans, for instance, some Christians were in the habit of worshipping at Muslim shrines, while some Muslims in their turn frequented Christian ones. Again, in the course of fighting the Turks in the sixteenth and seventeenth centuries, Poles and Hungarians adopted Turkish modes of fighting, such as the use of the scimitar, and it was they who introduced the Ottoman style of light cavalry to the rest of Europe in the form of regiments of lancers and hussars.

The epic and the ballad are genres that have flourished particularly on borders, between Christians and Muslims in Spain or Eastern Europe, for instance, or between the English and the Scots. The same stories of conflict have often been sung on both sides of the border, with the same protagonists (Roland, Johnnie Armstrong or Marko Kraljević), even if the heroes and the villains sometimes change places. In short, frontiers are often the scene of cultural encounters.

Interpreting cultural encounters

One reason that cultural history is unlikely to disappear, despite possible reactions against it, is the importance of cultural encounters in our time, generating an increasingly urgent need to understand them in the past.

The term 'cultural encounters' came into use to replace the ethnocentric word 'discovery', especially in the course of the commemoration in 1992 of the five hundredth anniversary of Columbus's landfall. It is associated with new perspectives in the history, with attention given to what the Mexican historian Miguel León-Portilla has called the 'vision of the vanquished' as well as that of the victors.[29] Historians have attempted to reconstruct the ways in which the Caribs perceived Columbus, the Aztecs Cortés, or the Hawaiians Captain Cook (the plural, 'ways', emphasizes the point that different Hawaiians, men and women, for instance, or chiefs and people, may have perceived the encounter differently).

A concern with misunderstanding is becoming increasingly central to studies of this kind, although the concept of 'misunderstanding', implying that there is a correct alternative, is often challenged. In its place we often see the employment of the term 'cultural translation'. The idea that understanding an alien culture was analogous to the work of translation first became current among anthropologists in the middle of the twentieth century in the circle of Edward Evans-Pritchard. Today, cultural historians are increasingly interested in the idea.

One situation in which it is particularly illuminating to think in these terms is the history of missions. When missionaries from Europe were attempting to convert the inhabitants of other continents to Christianity, they often tried to present their message in such a way that it would seem to be in harmony with the local culture. In other words, they believed Christianity to be translatable, and attempted to find local equivalents for ideas such as 'saviour', 'trinity', 'mother of God' and so on.

Receivers as well as donors engaged in the process of translation. Indigenous individuals and groups in China, Japan, Mexico, Peru, Africa and elsewhere who were attracted by particular items of western culture, from the mechanical clock to the art of perspective, have been described as 'translating' them in the sense of adapting them to their own cultures, taking them out of one context and inserting them into another. Interested as they usually were in discrete items rather than the structures in which those items were originally embedded, they practised a form of *bricolage*, whether literal, in the case of items of material culture, or metaphorical, in the case of ideas. Michel de Certeau's idea of 're-employment' (see pp. 77–8) seems particularly relevant here.

One example among many possible ones comes from nineteenth-century Africa, as described in a book by the British historian Gwyn Prins, *The Hidden Hippopotamus* (1980). Prins focuses on an encounter that took place in 1886 between the French Protestant missionary François Coillard and King Lewanika of Bulozi. Coillard, the founder of the Zambezi mission, saw himself as converting the 'heathen' and introducing a new belief system. However, on his way to meet the king, Coillard was asked to give a present of a metre of calico and he complied, without realizing that he would be perceived as sacrificing at a royal grave-site. This action turned him from a missionary into a chief and allowed Lewanika to relocate him in the local system.

An alternative concept, which has enjoyed considerable success in the last two decades, is that of cultural hybridity. The rival terms have their special advantages and disadvantages.

'Translation' has the advantage of emphasizing the work that has to be done by individuals and groups to domesticate the alien, the strategies and the tactics employed. The problem is that this work of domestication is not always conscious. When the Portuguese explorer Vasco da Gama and his men entered an Indian temple for the first time, they believed they were in a church and they 'saw' the Indian sculpture of Brahma Vishnu and Shiva as a representation of the Trinity. They were applying a perceptual schema from their own culture to interpret what they saw without realizing that they were doing so. Can we speak of unconscious translation?

The term 'hybridity', on the other hand, makes a space for these unconscious processes and unintended consequences. The weakness of this metaphor from botany is the opposite of its rival: it too easily gives the impression of a process that is smooth and 'natural', omitting human agency altogether.

A third model for cultural change comes from linguistics. In this age of cultural encounters, linguists have become increasingly interested in the process they describe as 'creolization', in other words the convergence of two languages to create a third, often taking most of its grammar from one and most of its vocabulary from the other. Cultural historians are coming to find this idea increasingly useful for analysing the consequences of encounters in the domains of religion, music, cuisine, clothing or even the sub-cultures of microphysics.[30]

Narrative in Cultural History

An encounter is an event, and so leads us to consider the possible place in cultural history of narratives of events, once associated with old-fashioned political history. A generation ago, the social historian Lawrence Stone noted with regret what he called 'the revival of narrative'. The trend he identified, however, might be described more precisely as a search for new forms of narrative in order to deal with social and cultural history.[31]

The story is a paradoxical one. Radical social historians rejected narrative because they associated it with an over-emphasis on the great deeds of great men, with the importance of individuals in history and especially the importance of political and military leaders being overestimated at the expense of ordinary men – and women. Yet narrative has returned together with an increasing concern with ordinary people and the ways in which they make sense of their experience, their lives, their world.

In the case of medicine, for instance, doctors now take more interest than before in the stories told by patients about their illnesses and their cures. In the case of the law, what is known as the 'legal storytelling movement' developed in the 1980s in the United States. The movement is linked to a concern with traditionally subordinate groups, especially ethnic minorities and women, because the stories told by members of these groups challenge a legal system which was created by white male lawyers who did not always have the needs and interests of other groups sufficiently in mind.

In similar fashion the current historical interest in narrative is in part an interest in the narrative practices characteristic of a particular culture, the stories that people in that culture 'tell themselves about themselves' (see p. 36). These 'cultural narratives', as they have been called, offer important clues to the world in which they were told. An intriguing and disturbing example comes from Russia, where the myth of the violent death of the tsar's son was played out four times in the early modern period, with the 'immolation' 'of Ivan by his father Ivan the Terrible, of Dimitri by Boris Godunov, of Alexis by Peter the Great, of Ivan by Catherine II'.[32]

There is also increasing interest in narrative as a historical force in its own right. Lynn Hunt's study of the French Revolution, discussed earlier, examined the 'narrative structures' underlying the rhetoric of the revolutionaries, the emplotment of the transition from the old regime to the new order either as comedy or as romance.

Recent studies of anti-Semitism in the Middle Ages by Ronnie Hsia and Miri Rubin have concentrated on the recurrent rumours accusing the Jews of desecrating the host and of the ritual murder of children, rumours which were gradually consolidated into a cultural narrative, discourse or myth. The stories helped to define a Christian identity, but they also constituted a 'narrative assault' on the Jews, a form of symbolic violence that led to real violence, to pogroms.[33] Stories about witches and their pacts with the devil could be analysed in similar terms.

Working on a later period, Judith Walkowitz is equally concerned with what she calls 'the narrative challenges raised by the new agenda of cultural history'. Her *City of Dreadful Delight* (1992) looked at late Victorian London through the lens of contemporary narratives, from the exposure of child prostitution in articles on 'The Maiden Tribute of Modern Babylon' to the reporting of the murders committed by 'Jack the Ripper'. These 'narratives of sexual danger' helped to produce an image of London as 'a dark, powerful and seductive labyrinth'. The stories drew on a cultural repertoire, but in turn they affected the perceptions of their readers.

Again, in *Islands of History* (1985) the anthropologist Marshall Sahlins has written about 'the distinctive role of the sign in action', adapting Kuhn's idea of a scientific paradigm challenged by new discoveries (see p. 49) to a cultural order challenged by an encounter, in this case the arrival of Captain Cook and his men in Hawaii. He shows the Hawaiians trying to fit Cook into their traditional narratives of the annual appearance of their god Lono, and attempting to deal with discrepancies between the two by adjusting the narrative.

An important implication of Sahlins's essay is that it is possible to write cultural history itself in a narrative form, very different from the relatively static 'portraits' of ages painted by Burckhardt and Huizinga. The challenge would be to do this without emplotting the story in either a triumphalist fashion, like the traditional textbooks of 'Western Civilization' as the story of progress, or in a tragic, nostalgic one, as the story of loss.

Civil wars, for instance, from seventeenth-century Britain to the nineteenth-century USA might be studied as cultural conflicts. A fascinating narrative history of the Spanish Civil War might be written from this point of view, presenting it as a series of collisions between regional cultures and class cultures as well as a conflict between opposed political ideals. Complex narratives expressing a multiplicity of viewpoints are a way of making conflict intelligible as well as resisting the tendency to fragmentation described earlier.

The example of China in the 1960s encouraged some historians to think about past 'cultural revolutions', notably in the case of France in 1789 with its new political culture (see p. 104) and the attempt of the regime to enforce an egalitarian uniformity in dress, replacing the hierarchical dress codes of the old regime. In similar fashion in the sphere of language, there was a plan to replace the local *patois*, or dialect, with French in order 'to melt the citizens into a national mass'.

Other revolutions also repay examination from this point of view. In the course of the Puritan Revolution, for instance, the theatres were closed and new naming practices adopted in some places, with names like 'Praise-God' symbolizing the parents' adherence to the new religious ideals. Again, the Bolshevik Revolution included a 'civilizing campaign'. Leon Trotsky, for instance, was concerned with 'cultured speech', making attempts to eliminate swearing and persuade officers in the army to use the polite form of address (*Vy*, like the French *vous*, rather than *Ty*, like *tu*), when speaking to their men. Special propaganda trains took revolutionary films, texts and songs to ordinary people all over Russia.[34]

A cultural history of revolutions should not assume that these events make everything new. As was noted above, apparent innovation may mask the persistence of tradition. There should be a place in the story for cultural survivals or even for what might be called the 'return of the repressed', visible in England in 1660 when the monarchy was restored and the playhouses reopened. There should also be a place for re-enactments. The leaders of one revolution have often seen themselves as re-enacting an earlier one. The Bolsheviks had their eyes on the French Revolution, for instance, the French revolutionaries thought of themselves as re-enacting the English Revolution, and the English in turn saw the events of their time as a replay of the French religious wars of the sixteenth century. The narratives written by cultural historians need to incorporate such views, without of course repeating them uncritically.

Re-enactments are not confined to revolutions. Within Christian culture, individuals have sometimes seen themselves as re-enacting Christ's Passion, from Thomas Becket in the days before his murder in Canterbury Cathedral to Patrick

Pearse organizing resistance to the British from the Dublin Post Office in 1916.

Again, in Sri Lanka today, some Sinhalese see themselves as re-enacting one of the religious narratives central to their culture, and they cast the Tamils in the role of demons. What Hayden White calls 'emplotment' (see p. 80) is to be found not only in the works of historians, but also in attempts by ordinary people to make sense of their world. Once again the importance of cultural or perceptual schemata is apparent, but in this case the schemata inform a narrative, a 'narrative assault' like the one against the Jews, destructive in its consequences. A history of Sri Lanka, whether cultural or political, needs to find a place for such a narrative, and also, of course, for the Tamil counter-narrative. In an age of ethnic conflicts, it is more than likely that we will be seeing more of this kind of history.

Conclusion

In the precise sense of the term, any 'conclusion' to this book would be out of place. The NCH may be coming to the end of its life-cycle, but the larger story of cultural history is still in progress. Some domains, such as the cultural history of language, are only now opening up to historical research. Current problems remain unsolved – at least, they have not been solved to everyone's satisfaction – and new problems are bound to arise. What follows, therefore, is not a formal conclusion but simply the expression of a few personal opinions, probably but not necessarily shared by colleagues.

In the last generation, cultural history – in the different senses of the term discussed earlier in this book – has been the arena in which some of the most exciting and illuminating discussions of historical method have taken place. At the same time, cultural historians, like social historians, have been extending the territory of the historian as well as making history more accessible to a wide public.

All the same, I have not argued here and do not in fact believe that cultural history is the best form of history. It is simply a necessary part of the collective historical enterprise.

Like its neighbours – economic history, political history, intellectual history, social history and so on – this approach to the past makes an indispensable contribution to our view of history as a whole, 'total history' as the French used to call it.

The recent fashion for cultural history has been a gratifying experience for practitioners like myself, but we know that cultural fashions do not last. Sooner or later there will be a reaction against 'culture'. When it comes, we have to do everything we can to ensure that recent gains in historical insight – results of the cultural turn – are not lost. Historians, especially empiricist or 'positivist' historians, used to suffer from the disease of literal-mindedness. Many of them were insufficiently sensitive to symbolism. Many of them treated historical documents as transparent, paying little or no attention to their rhetoric. Many of them dismissed certain human actions, such as blessing with two fingers or three (see p. 71) as 'mere' ritual, 'mere' symbols, matters of no importance.[35] In the last generation, cultural historians, like cultural anthropologists, have demonstrated the weaknesses of this positivist approach. Whatever the future of historical studies, there should be no return to literal-mindedness.

Notes

Introduction

1 Samuel P. Huntington, *The Clash of Civilizations and the Remaking of World Order* (New York, 1996); Jutta Scherrer, 'Kul'turologija', *Budapest Review of Books* 12: 1–2 (2003), 6–11.

Chapter 1 The Great Tradition

1 Peter Burke, 'Reflections on the Origins of Cultural History' (1991; repr. in *Varieties of Cultural History* (Cambridge, 1997)); Don Kelley, 'The Old Cultural History', *History and the Human Sciences*, 101–26.

2 The classic account of the English part of the story remains Raymond Williams, *Culture and Society* (1958). On the *Kulturkampf* (a term coined by Rudolf Virchow, an early student of anthropology), see Christopher Clark and Wolfram Kaiser (eds.), *Culture Wars: Secular-Catholic Conflict in Nineteenth-Century Europe* (Cambridge, 2003).

3 Francis Haskell, *History and its Images* (New Haven, 1993), 335–46, 482–94.

4 Lionel Gossmann, *Basel in the Age of Burckhardt* (Chicago, 2000), 226, 254.

5 Johan Huizinga, 'The Task of Cultural History', in *Men and Ideas* (New York, 1952), 77–96 and 17–76; *America* (New York, 1972), 192 (written in 1918).

6 Aby Warburg's essays have at last been translated into English under the title *Renewal of Pagan Antiquity* (Los Angeles, 1999).

7 Originally published in German in 1932 and in revised form in English in 1939, this essay is most accessible in Erwin Panofsky, *Meaning in the Visual Arts* (New York, 1957), 26–54.

8 Daniel Snowman, *The Hitler Emigrés: The Cultural Impact on Britain of Refugees from Nazism* (2002).

9 Gilbert Allardyce, 'The Rise and Fall of the Western Civilization Course', *American Historical Review* 87 (1982), 695–725; Daniel A. Segal, ' "Western Civ" and the Staging of History in American Higher Education', *American Historical Review* 105 (2000), 770–805.

10 Among Yates's most important books are *Giordano Bruno and the Hermetic Tradition* (1964) and *Astraea: the Imperial Theme in the Sixteenth Century* (1975).

11 Peter Burke, 'The Central European Moment in British Cultural Studies', in Herbert Grabes (ed.), *Literary History/Cultural History: Force-Fields and Tensions* (Tübingen, 2001), 279–88.

12 Frederick Antal, *Florentine Painting and its Social Background* (1947); *Hogarth and his Place in European Art* (1962).

13 Peter Burke, *Popular Culture in Early Modern Europe* (1978; revised edn. Aldershot, 1993), ch. 1.

Chapter 2   Problems of Cultural History

1 Jacob Burckhardt, *The Greeks and Greek Civilization*, ed. Oswyn Murray (1998), 5.

2 François Furet (ed.), *Livre et société dans la France du 18e siècle* (Paris-The Hague, 1965).

3 Bernard Cousin, *Le Miracle et le quotidien: les ex-voto provençaux images d'une société* (Aix, 1983).

4 See 'metus' and 'pavor' in Arnold Gerber and Adolf Graef, *Lexikon Taciteum* (Leipzig, 1903).

5 Régine Robin, *Histoire et linguistique* (Paris, 1973), 139–58.

6 Alexandra Georgakopoulou and Dionysis Goutsos, *Discourse Analysis: An Introduction* (Edinburgh, 1997).

7 Ernst Gombrich, 'In Search of Cultural History' (1969; repr. in *Ideals and Idols* (1979), 25–59).

8 Edward Thompson, 'Custom and Culture' (1978; repr. in *Customs in Common* (1993)).

9 Ernst Bloch, *Heritage of Our Times* (1935; English trans. Cambridge, 1991).

10 Raymond Williams, *Marxism and Literature* (Oxford, 1977).
11 Examples from China in Benjamin Schwartz, 'Some Polarities in Confucian Thought', in David S. Nivison and Arthur F. Wright (eds.), *Confucianism in Action* (Stanford, 1959), 50–62; from India in J. C. Heesterman, *The Inner Conflict of Traditions* (Chicago, 1985), 10–25.
12 Michel de Certeau, Jacques Revel and Dominique Julia, 'La Beauté du mort' (1970; repr. in Certeau, *La Culture au pluriel* (revised edn. Paris, 1993), 45–72); Stuart Hall, 'Notes on Deconstructing the "Popular"', in Raphael Samuel (ed.), *People's History and Socialist Theory* (1981), 227–40; Roger Chartier, *Cultural History* (Cambridge, 1988), 37–40.
13 John J. Winkler, *The Constraints of Desire: The Anthropology of Sex and Gender in Ancient Greece* (1990), especially 162–209.
14 Chartier, *Cultural History*; Peter Burke, *Popular Culture in Early Modern Europe* (1987; revised edn. Aldershot, 1993).
15 Georges Duby, 'The Diffusion of Cultural Patterns in Feudal Society', *Past and Present* 39 (1968), 1–10.

Chapter 3 The Moment of Historical Anthropology

1 For the situation in political science, see the forthcoming book by Patrick Chabal and Jean-Pascal Daloz, *Culture Troubles: Comparative Politics and the Interpretation of Meaning*.
2 Michael Bellesiles, *Arming America: The Origins of a National Gun Culture* (New York, 2000).
3 Keith Thomas, 'Ways of Doing Cultural History', in *Balans and Perspectief van de nederlandse cultuurgeschiedenis*, ed. Rik Sanders et al. (Amsterdam, 1991), 65.
4 Martin J. Wiener, *English Culture and the Decline of the Industrial Spirit, 1850–1980* (Cambridge, 1981); David Landes, *The Wealth and Poverty of Nations* (1998); Eric Van Young, 'The New Cultural History Comes to Old Mexico', *Hispanic American Historical Review* 79 (1999), 211–48, at 238; Erik Ringmar, *Identity, Interest and Action: A Cultural Explanation of Sweden's Intervention in the Thirty Years War* (Cambridge, 1996).
5 Aaron Gurevich, 'Wealth and Gift-Bestowal among the ancient Scandinavians' (1968; repr. in his *Historical Anthropology of the Middle Ages* (Cambridge, 1992), 177–89). Cf Natalie Z. Davis, *The Gift in Sixteenth-Century France* (Oxford, 2000).

6   Keith Thomas, *Religion and the Decline of Magic* (1971), especially 216–17, 339, 463n, 566, 645; cf. Maria Lúcia Pallares-Burke, *The New History: Confessions and Conversations* (Cambridge, 2002).

7   Anton Blok, 'Infamous Occupations', in *Honour and Violence* (Cambridge, 2001), 44–68.

8   Natalie Z. Davis, 'The Rites of Violence' (1973; repr. in *Society and Culture in Early Modern France* (Stanford, 1975)), 152–88.

9   Juri M. Lotman, 'The Poetics of Everyday Behaviour in Russian Eighteenth-Century Culture', in Lotman and Boris A. Uspenskii, *The Semiotics of Russian Culture* (Ann Arbor, 1984), 231–56; cf id., *Russlands Adel: Eine Kulturgeschichte von Peter I. bis Nikolaus I.* (1994; German trans. Köln, 1997).

10 Clifford Geertz, *The Interpretation of Cultures* (New York, 1973), 3–30; the definition is given on p. 89.

11 Ibid., 412–53.

12 Victor Turner, *Schism and Continuity in African Society* (Manchester, 1957), 91–3, 230–2.

13 Clifford Geertz, *Negara: The Theatre State in Nineteenth-Century Bali* (Princeton, 1980).

14 Roger Chartier, 'Texts, Symbols and Frenchness: Historical Uses of Symbolic Anthropology' (1985; repr. in *Cultural History*, 95–111).

15 Stephen Greenblatt, *Shakespearian Negotiations* (Oxford, 1988).

16 Cf. Natalie Davis in Maria Lúcia Pallares-Burke (ed.), *The New History: Confessions and Conversations* (Cambridge, 2002), 50–79.

17 Johan Huizinga, 'My Path to History', in *Dutch Civilisation in the 17th Century and Other Essays*, ed. Pieter Geyl and F. W. N. Hugenholtz (1968).

18 Troels-Lund's work is regrettably unavailable in English, but it is discussed in Bjarne Stoklund, *Folklife Research between History and Anthropology* (Cardiff, 1983).

19 Thomas, 'Cultural History', 74.

20 Among the most penetrating accounts are Giovanni Levi, 'Micro-history', in Peter Burke (ed.), *New Perspectives on Historical Writing* (1991; 2nd edn. Cambridge, 2001), 97–119, and Jacques Revel (ed.), *Jeux d'échelle* (Paris, 1996).

21 Charles Phythian-Adams, 'An Agenda for English Local History', in *Societies, Cultures and Kinship* (Leicester, 1993), 1–23; David Underdown, 'Regional Cultures?' in Tim Harris (ed.), *Popular Culture in England c. 1500–1850* (1995), 28–47.

22 Hans Medick, *Weben und Überleben in Laichingen, 1650–1900. Lokalgeschichte als Allgemeine Geschichte* (Göttingen, 1996).

23 Robert J. C. Young, *Postcolonialism: An Historical Introduction* (Oxford, 2001).

24 For a critical reaction to Said's central thesis, see John M. MacKenzie, *Orientalism: History, Theory and the Arts* (Manchester, 1995). Cf. W. J. McCormack, *Ascendancy and Tradition* (Oxford, 1985), 219–38, on 'Celticism', and James Carrier (ed.), *Occidentalism: Images of the West* (Oxford, 1995).

25 See Joan Kelly, *Women, History and Theory* (Chicago, 1984). The article was first published in 1977.

26 Examples of the trends discussed above include Patricia Labalme (ed.), *Beyond their Sex: Learned Women of the European Past* (New York, 1980); Catherine King, *Renaissance Women Patrons* (Manchester, 1988); Lorna Hutson (ed.), *Feminism and Renaissance Studies* (Oxford, 1999); Letitia Panizza and Sharon Wood (eds.), *A History of Women's Writing in Italy* (Cambridge, 2000).

Chapter 4 A New Paradigm?

1 Thomas Kuhn, *The Structure of Scientific Revolutions* (Chicago, 1962), 10.

2 Thomas Bender and Carl E. Schorske (eds.), *Budapest and New York: Studies in Metropolitan Transformation* (New York, 1994); Robert B. St George (ed.), *Possible Pasts: Becoming Colonial in Early America* (Ithaca, 2000).

3 For the debate, see Craig Calhoun (ed.), *Habermas and the Public Sphere* (Cambridge, MA, 1992). Cf. Joan Landes, *Women and the Public Sphere in the Age of the French Revolution* (Ithaca, 1988); Thomas F. Crow, *Painters and Public Life in Eighteenth-Century Paris* (Princeton, 1985); Brendan Dooley and Sabrina Baron (eds.), *The Politics of Information in Early Modern Europe* (2001).

4 Joan Scott, 'Women's History', in Peter Burke (ed.), *New Perspectives on Historical Writing* (1991; 2nd edn. Cambridge, 2001), 43–70, at 50–1; Stuart Clark, *Thinking with Demons* (Oxford, 1997), 143.

5 Mikhail Bakhtin, *Rabelais and his World* (1965; English trans. Cambridge, MA, 1968); id, *The Dialogic Imagination* (Manchester, 1981); Robert W. Scribner, *Popular Culture and Popular Movements in Reformation Germany* (1987), 95–7;

Peter Burke, 'Bakhtin for Historians', *Social History* 13 (1988), 85–90.

6 Michel Foucault, *Madness and Civilization* (1961; English trans. 1965); *The Order of Things* (1966; English trans. 1970); *Discipline and Punish* (1975; English trans. 1979); *History of Sexuality* (3 vols, 1976–84; English trans. 1984–8). For an assessment, see David C. Hoy (ed.), *Foucault: A Critical Reader* (Oxford, 1986).

7 Pierre Bourdieu, *Outlines of a Theory of Practice* (1972; English trans. Cambridge, 1977); id, *Distinction* (1979; English trans. 1984); on him, David Swartz, *Culture and Power, The Sociology of Pierre Bourdieu* (Chicago, 1997).

8 This is Bourdieu's own account, in a conversation I had with him *c*.1982. It has been pointed out that the term 'habitus' was also used by Leibniz, whose philosophy Bourdieu studied at the Ecole Normale.

9 Peter Burke and Roy Porter (eds.), *The Social History of Language* (Cambridge, 1987).

10 Ruth Harris, *Lourdes: Body and Spirit in a Secular Age* (1999); Victor Turner and Edith Turner, *Image and Pilgrimage in Western Culture* (Oxford, 1978).

11 Jaś Elsner and Joan-Pau Rubiès (eds.), *Voyages and Visions: Towards a Cultural History of Travel* (1999).

12 Jaś Elsner and Roger Cardinal (eds.), *The Cultures of Collecting* (1994).

13 Steven Shapin and Simon Schaffer, *Leviathan and the Air-Pump* (Princeton, 1985).

14 Roger Chartier, *The Cultural Uses of Print in Early Modern France* (Princeton, 1987); Guglielmo Cavallo and Roger Chartier (eds.), *A History of Reading in the West* (1995; English trans. Cambridge, 1999); Hans-Robert Jauss, *Towards an Aesthetic of Reception* (1974; English trans. Minneapolis, 1982); Wolfgang Iser, *The Act of Reading* (1976; English trans. 1978).

15 Robert Darnton, 'Readers Respond to Rousseau', in his *Great Cat Massacre* (New York, 1984), 215–56; James Raven, Helen Small and Naomi Tadmor (eds.), *The Practice and Representation of Reading in England* (Cambridge, 1996; John Brewer's essay is on pp. 226–45).

16 Erich Schön, *Der Verlust der Sinnlichkeit oder Die Verwandlungen des Lesers: Mentalitätswandel um 1800* (Stuttgart, 1987).

17 Peter Kornicki, *The Book in Japan: A Cultural History from the Beginnings to the Nineteenth Century* (Leiden, 1998);

Stephen Lovell, *The Russian Reading Revolution: Print Culture in the Soviet and Post-Soviet Eras* (Basingstoke, 2000).

18 Jacques Le Goff, 'Dreams in the Culture and Collective Psychology of the Medieval West' (1971; English trans. in his *Time, Work and Culture in the Middle Ages* (Chicago, 1980), 201–4).

19 William A. Christian, Jr, *Apparitions in Late Medieval and Renaissance Spain* (Princeton, 1981); Jean-Claude Schmitt, *Ghosts* (1994; English trans. 1998).

20 Michael Gilsenan, quoted in Peter Burke, 'How to be a Counter-Reformation Saint', in *Historical Anthropology of Early Modern Italy* (Cambridge, 1987), 48–62, at p. 53.

21 Linda Nochlin, 'The Imaginary Orient' (1983; repr. in her *Politics of Vision* (New York, 1989), 33–59); James Thompson, *The East Imagined, Experienced, Remembered: Orientalist 19th-Century Painting* (Dublin and Liverpool, 1988); Edward Said, *Culture and Imperialism* (1993), 134–57.

22 Ralph P. Locke, 'Constructing the Oriental "Other": Saint-Saëns's *Samson et Dalila*', *Cambridge Opera Journal* 3 (1991), 261–303.

23 Richard Taruskin, 'Entoiling the Falconet: Russian Musical Orientalism in Context' (1992; repr. in Jonathan Bellman (ed.), *The Exotic in Western Music* (Boston, 1998), 194–217).

24 For a survey of recent work, see Kerwin L. Klein, 'On the Emergence of Memory in Historical Discourse', *Representations* 69 (2000), 127–50. The abbreviated English translation of Nora's book is entitled *Realms of Memory* (3 vols, New York, 1996–8).

25 Philippe Joutard, *La Légende des Camisards* (Paris, 1977).

26 Paul Fussell, *The Great War and Modern Memory* (Oxford, 1975), 137, 317.

27 Ian McBride (ed.) *History and Memory in Modern Ireland* (Cambridge, 2001).

28 See Maria Lúcia Pallares-Burke, *The New History: Confessions and Conversations* (Cambridge, 2002), 116–19.

29 Roy Porter, 'History of the Body Reconsidered', in Peter Burke (ed.), *New Perspectives on Historical Writing* (1991; 2nd edn. Cambridge, 2001), 233–60.

30 G. Freyre, *O escravo nos anúncios de jornais brasileiros do século xix* (Recife, 1963); Jean-Pierre Aron, Pierre Dumond and Emmanuel Le Roy Ladurie, *Anthropologie du conscrit français* (The Hague, 1972).

31 Jan Bremmer and Herman Roodenburg (eds.), *The Cultural*

History of Gesture (Cambridge, 1991); Jean-Claude Schmitt, *La Raison des gestes dans l'occident médiéval* (Paris, 1990).

32   In Pallares-Burke, *New History*, 163.

33   William Sewell, 'The Concept (s) of Culture', in Victoria Bonnell and Lynn Hunt (eds.), *Beyond the Cultural Turn* (Berkeley, 1999), 35–61.

Chapter 5   From Representation to Construction

1   Chartier's remark, originally made at conferences, was eventually published in his 'Le Monde comme représentation', *Annales: economies, sociétés, civilisations* 44 (1989), 1505–20. Jan Golinski, *Making Natural Knowledge: Constructivism and the History of Science* (Cambridge, 1998); Ian Hacking, *The Social Construction of What?* (Cambridge, MA, 1999).

2   See Richard Rorty, *Philosophy and the Mirror of Nature* (Oxford, 1980).

3   Jim Sharpe, 'History from Below', in *New Perspectives on Historical Writing*, ed. Peter Burke (1991; second edn. Cambridge, 2001), 25–42; Nathan Wachtel, *Vision of the Vanquished: The Conquest of Peru through Indian Eyes* (1972; English trans. Cambridge, 1977).

4   For introductions to Certeau's work, see Jeremy Ahearne, *Michel de Certeau: Interpretation and its Other* (Cambridge, 1995), and Roger Chartier, *On the Edge of the Cliff* (Baltimore, 1997).

5   Michel de Certeau, Dominique Julia and Jacques Revel, *Une Politique de la langue: La Révolution Française et les patois* (Paris, 1975).

6   Michel de Certeau, *The Practice of Everyday Life* (1980; English trans. Berkeley, 1984).

7   Northrop Frye, 'New Directions for Old' (1960; repr. in his *Fables of Identity* (New York, 1963), 52–66).

8   Ronald Inden, 'Orientalist Constructions of India', *Modern Asian Studies* 20 (1986), 401–46; *Imagining India* (Oxford, 1990); Nicholas Dirks, *Castes of Mind: Colonialism and the Making of Modern India* (Princeton, 2001); Adrian Southall, 'The Illusion of Tribe', *Journal of African and Asian Studies* (1970), 28–50; and Jean-Loup Amselle, *Mestizo Logics: Anthropology of Identity in Africa and Elsewhere* (1990; English trans. Stanford, 1998).

9   Gareth Stedman Jones, *Languages of Class* (Cambridge, 1983), 101; cf. David Feldman, 'Class', in Peter Burke (ed.), *History and Historians in the Twentieth Century* (2002), 201–6.

10 Anton Blok, 'The Narcissism of Minor Differences' (1998; repr. in *Honour and Violence* (Cambridge, 2001), 115–31); Anthony P. Cohen, *The Symbolic Construction of Community* (Chichester, 1985).

11 Catherine Bell, *Ritual Theory, Ritual Practice* (New York, 1992).

12 Erik Lönnroth, *Den stora rollen: kung Gustav III spelad af honom själv* (Stockholm, 1986).

13 James S. Amelang, *The Flight of Icarus: Artisan Autobiography in Early Modern Europe* (Stanford, 1998).

14 Roy Foster, *W. B. Yeats* (Oxford, 1997), 90, 100, 141, 345, 373, 492, 512, 515, 526–8. Cf Richard Ellmann, *Yeats: The Man and the Masks* (1949).

15 Rudolf M. Dekker and Lotte van de Pol, *The Tradition of Female Transvestism in Early Modern Europe* (1989); Elaine K. Ginsberg (ed.), *Passing and the Fictions of Identity* (Durham, NC, 1996).

16 Richard M. Swiderski, *The False Formosan: George Psalmanazar and the Eighteenth-Century Experiment of Identity* (San Francisco, 1991), 252.

17 Marshall Sahlins, *Islands of History* (Chicago, 1985); John Austin, *How to Do Things with Words* (Oxford, 1962).

18 On historians and speech acts, see James Tully (ed.), *Meaning and Context: Quentin Skinner and His Critics* (Cambridge, 1988), and Maria Lúcia Pallares-Burke, *The New History: Confessions and Conversations* (Cambridge, 2002), 212–40.

19 Gilliam McIntosh, *The Force of Culture: Unionist Identities in 20th-Century Ireland* (Cork, 1999), 103–43; David M. Guss, *The Festive State: Race, Ethnicity and Nationalism as Cultural Performance* (Berkeley, 2000), 24–59; Neil Jarman, *Material Conflicts* (Oxford, 1997), 1–21; Rudolf Braun and David Gugerli, *Macht des Tanzes – Tanz der Mächtigen: Hoffeste und Herrschaftszeremoniell, 1550–1914* (Munich, 1993); Audrée-Isabelle Tardif, 'Social Dancing in England 1660–1815', Cambridge Ph.D thesis, completed 2002.

20 Michael Herzfeld, *The Poetics of Manhood* (Princeton, 1985), 51, 155.

21 James S. Scott, *Domination and the Arts of Resistance* (New Haven, 1990), 11. The book focuses on the discrepancy between public performances and private attitudes ('hidden transcripts').

22 Robert Le Page and Andrée Tabouret-Keller, *Acts of Identity* (Cambridge, 1985); James Fernandez, 'The Performance of Ritual Metaphors', in J. David Sapir and J. Christopher

Crocker (eds.), *The Social Use of Metaphor* (Philadelphia, 1977), 1–31.

23 Richard Krautheimer, *The Rome of Alexander VII* (Princeton, 1985), 4–6; Christopher Heuer, 'The City Rehearsed: Hans Vredemann de Vries and the Performance of Architecture', Ph.D thesis, Berkeley, in progress.

24 An attempt to use this approach in the study of popular performances is Peter Burke, *Popular Culture in Early Modern Europe* (1978), 124–36.

25 An early example is Robert W. Scribner, 'Oral Culture and the Diffusion of Reformation Ideas' (1984; repr. in his *Popular Culture and Popular Movements in Reformation Germany* (1990), 49–70). For an overview of recent work on Britain, see Adam Fox and Daniel Woolf (eds.), *The Spoken Word: Oral Culture in Britain, 1500–1850* (Manchester, 2003).

26 Thomas W. Laqueur, 'Crowds, Carnival and the State in English Executions, 1604–1868', in *The First Modern Society*, ed. A. Lee Beier and David Cannadine (Oxford, 1989), 305–55.

27 Peter Burke, *Historical Anthropology of Early Modern Italy* (Cambridge, 1987), 176–7; I have added a few more details from the diary.

28 Thomas Kaufmann, *Court, Cloister and City: The Art and Culture of Central Europe, 1450–1800* (1995), especially 57–73, 89–92.

29 F. W. Maitland, *The Constitutional History of England* (1888; posthumously published, Cambridge, 1908), 142.

30 L. Febvre, *Life in Renaissance France* (1925; English trans. Cambridge, MA, 1977).

31 Benjamin Schwartz, 'Some Polarities in Confucian Thought', in David Nivison and Arthur Wright (eds.), *Confucianism in Action* (Chicago, 1959), 50–62; J. C. Heesterman 'India and the Inner Conflict of Tradition' (1973; repr. in *The Inner Conflict of Traditions* (Chicago, 1985), 10–25).

Chapter 6 Beyond the Cultural Turn?

1 Peter Burke, 'Anthropology of the Renaissance', *Journal of the Institute for Romance Studies* 1 (1992), 207–15; *The European Renaissance: Centres and Peripheries* (Oxford, 1998), especially ch. 5.

2 Daryle Williams, *Culture Wars in Brazil: The First Vargas Regime, 1930–45* (Durham, NC, 2001).

3 Good examples of the group's work are collected in Ranajit Guha and Gayatri Chakravorty Spivak, *Selected Subaltern Studies* (New York, 1988). For the debate, see Vinayak Chaturvedi (ed.), *Mapping Subaltern Studies and the Post-colonial* (2000).

4 Shahid Amin, 'Gandhi as Mahatma', in Guha and Spivak, *Studies*, 288–348.

5 On Latin America, see John Beverley, *Subalternity and Representation* (Durham, NC, 1999); cf. David Lloyd, 'Irish New Histories and the "Subalternity Effect"', *Subaltern Studies* 9 (1996), 261–77.

6 Joad Raymond, *The Invention of the Newspaper: English Newsbooks 1641–1649* (Oxford, 1996); Alastair Bellany, *The Politics of Court Scandal in Early Modern England: News Culture and the Overbury Affair, 1603–1660* (Cambridge, 2002).

7 Olivier Ihl, *La Fête républicaine* (Paris, 1996); Matthew Truesdell, *Spectacular Politics:* Louis Napoléon *and the fête impériale, 1849–70* (New York, 1997); Lucien Bély, *Espions et ambassadeurs au temps de Louis XIV* (Paris, 1990), especially part 2, offers a cultural history of diplomacy around the year 1700.

8 John Keegan, *A History of Warfare* (1993), 3–12; Joanna Bourke, *Dismembering the Male: Men's Bodies, Britain and the Great War* (1996); Benigna von Krusenstjern and Hans Medick (eds.), *Zwischen Alltag und Katatrophe: Der Dreissigjährige Krieg aus der Nahe* (Göttingen, 1999).

9 Robert Wohl, *The Generation of 1914* (Cambridge, MA, 1979); Modris Eksteins, *Rites of Spring: The Great War and the Birth of the Modern Age* (1989); Jay Winter, *Sites of Memory, Sites of Mourning: The Great War in European Cultural History* (Cambridge, 1998).

10 Charles Coulson, 'Cultural Realities and Reappraisals in English Castle Studies', *Journal of Medieval History* 22 (1996), 171–207; on naval spectacles, see Jan Rüger's Cambridge Ph.D thesis (2002).

11 Keith Baker, *Inventing the French Revolution* (Chicago, 1990), 13; Bertram Wyatt Brown, *Southern Honour* (New York, 1982); Peter Burke, 'The Virgin of the Carmine and the Revolt of Masaniello' (1983; repr. in *Historical Anthropology of Early Modern Italy* (Cambridge, 1987), 191–206); and, more generally, Anton Blok, 'The Meaning of "Senseless" Violence', in *Honour and Violence* (Cambridge, 2001), 103–14.

12 Natalie Z. Davis, 'The Rites of Violence' (1973; repr. in *Society and Culture in Early Modern France* (Stanford, 1975), 152–88;

cf. Maria Lúcia Pallares-Burke, *The New History: Confessions and Conversations* (Cambridge, 2002); Janine Garrisson-Estèbe, *Tocsin pour un massacre* (Paris, 1968); Emmanuel Le Roy Ladurie, *Carnival: A People's Uprising at Romans, 1579–1580* (1979; English trans. 1980); Denis Crouzet, *Les Guerriers de Dieu* (Paris, 1990).

13 David Niremberg, *Communities of Violence: Persecution of Minorities in the Middle Ages* (Princeton, 1996).

14 A few weeks after first writing these lines, a special issue of *Annales: histoire, sciences sociales* appeared (in 2002), on the theme of 'culture de la terreur', concentrating on the French Revolution.

15 Peter Burke, 'Is there a Cultural History of the Emotions?' in Penelope Gouk and Helen Hills (eds.), *Representing Emotions* (2003).

16 Anne Vincent-Buffault, *The History of Tears* (1986; English trans. 1991); Piroska Nagy, *Le Don des larmes au Moyen Age* (Paris, 2000); Lynn Hunt and Margaret Jacob, 'The Affective Revolution in 1790s' Britain', *Eighteenth-Century Studies* 34 (2001), 491–521.

17 Theodore Zeldin, *France 1848–1945* (2 vols, Oxford, 1973–7); Peter Gay, *The Bourgeois Experience* (5 vols, New York 1984–).

18 Hans J. Rindisbacher, *The Smell of Books: A Cultural-Historical Study of Olfactory Perception in Literature* (Ann Arbor, 1992); Constance Classen, David Howes and Anthony Synnott, *Aroma: the Cultural History of Smell* (1994); Mark Jenner, 'Civilization and Deodorization? Smell in Early Modern English Culture', in Peter Burke, Brian Harrison and Paul Slack (eds.), *Civil Histories: Essays Presented to Sir Keith Thomas* (Oxford, 2000), 127–44; Robert Jütte, *A History of the Senses* (Cambridge, 2004).

19 Peter Bailey, 'Breaking the Sound Barrier: A Historian Listens to Noise', *Body and Society* 2 (1996), 49–66; Bruce R. Smith, *The Acoustic World of Early Modern England* (Chicago, 1999); Jean-Pierre Gutton, *Bruits et sons dans notre histoire* (Paris, 2000); Emily Cockayne, 'Sound in Early Modern England', Ph.D thesis, Cambridge 2000.

20 Stephen Haber, 'Anything Goes: Mexico's "New" Cultural History', *Hispanic American Historical Review* 79 (1999), 309–30. Other articles in the same issue continue the debate.

21 Victoria E. Bonnell and Lynn Hunt (eds.), *Beyond the Cultural Turn* (Berkeley, 1999), 1–32.

22 An attempt to work out these rules may be found in Peter Burke, *Eyewitnessing* (2001).

23 Philippe Buc, *The Dangers of Ritual* (Princeton, 2001).
24 Michael Kammen, 'Extending the Reach of American Cultural History' (1984; repr. in *Selvages and Biases* (Ithaca, 1987), 118–53); cf. Thomas Bender, 'Wholes and Parts: the Need for Synthesis in American History', *Journal of American History* 73 (1986), 120–36.
25 Frank R. Ankersmit, 'Historiography and Postmodernism', *History and Theory* 28 (1989), 137–53; Ginzburg's reaction in Maria Lúcia Pallares-Burke (ed.), *The New History: Confessions and Conversations* (Cambridge, 2002), 205.
26 Among the many recent studies, see Peter Sahlins, *Boundaries: The Making of France and Spain in the Pyrenees* (Berkeley, 1989); Mary Louis Pratt, *Imperial Eyes: Travel Writing and Transculturation* (1992); Robert Bartlett, *The Making of Europe: Conquest, Colonization and Cultural Change* (1993), 950–1350.
27 Peter Burke, 'Civilizations and Frontiers: The Anthropology of the Early Modern Mediterranean', in John A. Marino (ed.), *Early Modern History and the Social Sciences: Testing the Limits of Braudel's Mediterranean* (Kirksville, 2002), 123–41.
28 T. F. Carter, 'Islam as a Barrier to Printing', *The Moslem World* 33 (1943), 213–16; Brinkley Messick, *The Calligraphic State: Textual Domination and History in a Muslim Society* (Berkeley, 1993); Francis Robinson, 'Islam and the Impact of Print in South Asia', in Nigel Crook (ed.), *The Transmission of Knowledge in South Asia* (Delhi, 1996), 62–97.
29 The phrase was borrowed by the French historian Nathan Wachtel for the title of his important study of colonial Peru: *Vision of the Vanquished: The Spanish Conquest of Peru through Indian Eyes, 1530–1570* (1971; English trans. Hassocks, 1977).
30 Peter Galison, *Image and Logic: A Material Culture of Microphysics* (Chicago, 1997); David Buisseret and Steven G. Reinhardt (eds.), *Creolization in the Americas* (Arlington, 2000).
31 Lawrence Stone, 'The Revival of Narrative', *Past and Present* 85 (1979), 3–24; Peter Burke, 'History of Events and Revival of Narrative', in Burke (ed.), *New Perspectives on Historical Writing* (1991; 2nd edn. Cambridge, 2001), 283–300.
32 Alain Besançon, *Le Tsarévich immolé* (Paris, 1967), 78; Sarah Maza, 'Stories in History: Cultural Narratives in Recent Works in European History', *American Historical Review* 101 (1996), 1493–1515; Karen Halttunen, 'Cultural History and the Challenge of Narrativity', in Victoria Bonnell and Lynn Hunt (eds.), *Beyond the Cultural Turn* (Berkeley, 1999), 165–81.

33   Ronnie Hsia, *The Myth of Ritual Murder* (New Haven, 1988); Miri Rubin, *Gentile Tales* (New Haven, 1999).

34   Peter Kenez, *Birth of the Propaganda State: Soviet Methods of Mass Mobilization, 1917–1929* (Cambridge, 1985).

35   Peter Burke, 'The Repudiation of Ritual in Early Modern Europe', in *Historical Anthropology of Early Modern Europe* (Cambridge, 1987), 223–38; 'The Rise of Literal-Mindedness', *Common Knowledge* 2, 2 (1993), 108–21.

Select Publications on Cultural History, 1860–2003: A Chronological List

Needless to say, this is a personal selection.

1860 Burckhardt, *Kultur der Renaissance in Italien*
1894 Troels-Lund, *Om kulturhistorie*
1897 Lamprecht, 'Was ist Kulturgeschichte?'
1904 Weber, *Protestantische Ethik*
1919 Huizinga, *Herfsttij der Middeleeuwen*
1927 Beard and Beard, *Rise of American Civilization*
1932 Dawson, *Making of Europe*
1932 Warburg, *Die Erneuerung der heidnischer Antike*
1933 Freyre, *Casa Grande e Senzala*
1934 Willey, *Seventeenth-Century Background*
1936 Young, *Victorian England*
1939 Elias, *Über den Prozess der Zivilisation*
1942 Febvre, *Problème de l'incroyance*
1947 Klingender, *Art and the Industrial Revolution*
1948 Castro, *España en su historia*
1948 Curtius, *Europäisches Literatur und lateinisches Mittelalter*
1948 Giedion, *Mechanization Takes Command*
1951 Panofsky, *Gothic Architecture and Scholasticism*
1954 Needham, *Science and Civilization in China*
1958 Williams, *Culture and Society*
1959 Hobsbawm, *Jazz Scene*
1959 León-Portilla, *Visión de los vencidos*
1959 Smith, *European Vision and the South Pacific*
1960 Lord, *Singer of Tales*

1963 Thompson, *Making of the English Working Class*
1965 Bakhtin, *Tvorchestvo Fransua Rable*
1965 Dodds, *Pagan and Christian in an Age of Anxiety*
1967 Braudel, *Civilisation matérielle et capitalisme*
1971 Thomas, *Religion and the Decline of Magic*
1971 Wachtel, *La Vision des vaincus*
1972 Baxandall, *Painting and Experience in Fifteenth-Century Italy*
1972 Burke, *Culture and Society in Renaissance Italy*
1973–7 Zeldin, *France 1848–1945*
1973 White, *Metahistory*
1975 Certeau, *Une Politique de la langue*
1975 Davis, *Society and Culture in Early Modern France*
1975 Foucault, *Surveiller et punir*
1975 Le Roy Ladurie, *Montaillou*
1976 Ginzburg, *Il formaggio e I vermi*
1978 Burke, *Popular Culture in Early Modern Europe*
1978 Duby, *Les Trois Ordres*
1978 Said, *Orientalism*
1978 Skinner, *Foundations of Modern Political Thought*
1979 Frykman and Löfgren, *Kultiverade människan*
1979 Lyons, *Culture and Anarchy in Ireland*
1979 Schorske, *Fin-de-Siècle Vienna*
1980 Brown and Elliott, *A Palace for a King*
1980 Greenblatt, *Renaissance Self-Fashioning*
1981 Gurevich, *Problemy srvednovekovoi narodnoi*
1981 Le Goff, *Naissance du Purgatoire*
1981 Wiener, *English Culture and the Decline of the Industrial Spirit*
1982 Corbin, *Le Miasme et la jonquille*
1982 Isaac, *Transformation of Virginia*
1982 Wyatt-Brown, *Southern Honor*
1983 Anderson, *Imagined Communities*
1983 Hobsbawm and Ranger (eds.), *Invention of Tradition*
1984 Darnton, *Great Cat Massacre*
1984 Gay, *Bourgeois Experience*
1984 Hunt, *Politics, Culture and Class in the French Revolution*
1984–93 Nora (ed.), *Lieux de Mémoire*
1985 Jouhaud, *Mazarinades*
1985 Mintz, *Sweetness and Power*

1985 Sahlins, *Islands of History*
1986 McKenzie, *Bibliography and the Sociology of Texts*
1987 Bynum, *Holy Feast and Holy Fast*
1987 Campbell, *Romantic Ethic and Spirit of Consumerism*
1987 Davis, *Fiction in the Archives*
1987 Schama, *Embarrassment of Riches*
1987 Schön, *Verlust der Sinnlichkeit*
1988 Briggs, *Victorian Things*
1988 Brown, *Body and Society*
1988 Chartier, *Cultural History*
1988 Greenblatt, *Shakespearian Negotiations*
1988 Gruzinski, *La Colonisation de l'imaginaire*
1988 Guha and Spivak (eds.), *Selected Subaltern Studies*
1988 Mitchell, *Colonising Egypt*
1989 Fischer, *Albion's Seed*
1989 Freedberg, *Power of Images*
1989 Hunt (ed.), *New Cultural History*
1989 Roche, *Culture des apparences*
1990 Crouzet, *Guerriers de Dieu*
1990 Porter, *Mind-Forg'd Manacles*
1990 Winkler, *Constraints of Desire*
1991 Clunas, *Superfluous Things*
1992 Burke, *Fabrication of Louis XIV*
1992 Walkowitz, *City of Dreadful Delight*
1993 Bartlett, *Making of Europe*
1993 Brewer and Porter (eds.), *Consumption and the World of Goods*
1994 Corbin, *Les Cloches de la terre*
1994 Schmitt, *Histoire des revenants*
1994 Shapin, *Social History of Truth*
1994 Stearns and Stearns, *American Cool*
1995 Wortman, *Scenarios of Power*
1996 Fujitani, *Splendid Monarchy*
1997 Brewer, *Pleasures of the Imagination*
1999 Hunt and Bonnell (eds.), *Beyond the Cultural Turn*
1999 Rubin, *Gentile Tales*
2000 Bellesisles, *Arming America*
2000 Burke, *Social History of Knowledge*
2000 St George (ed.), *Possible Pasts*
2001 Reddy, *Navigation of Feeling*
2003 Clark (ed.), *Culture Wars*

Further Reading

On concepts of culture and the history of cultural history, compare Raymond Williams, *Culture and Society* (1958) with Peter Burke, *Varieties of Cultural History* (Cambridge, 1997) and Adam Kuper, *Culture: the Anthropologist's Account* (Cambridge, MA, 1999).

On particular topics discussed in the course of this book, the examples cited in the text and the footnotes should be taken as suggestions for further reading.

The following fourteen titles constitutes a small selection of first-rate works published since 1980, available in English and ranging widely in space, time and theme.

Keith Baker, *Inventing the French Revolution* (Cambridge, 1990). A collection of distinguished essays in the style of the NCH.

Robert Bartlett, *The Making of Europe: Conquest, Colonization and Cultural Change, 950–1350* (1993). An ambitious and original study of the cultural consequences of the expansion of Europe's frontiers.

Hans Belting, *Likeness and Presence: A History of the Image Before the Era of Art* (1990; English trans. Chicago, 1994). An art historian historicizes the notion of art.

John Brewer, *The Pleasures of the Imagination: English Culture in the Eighteenth Century* (London, 1997). A perceptive social history of English culture in the age of its first commercialization.

Peter Brown, *The Body and Society: Men, Women and Sexual Renunciation in Early Christianity* (1988). A highly original study by one of the most distinguished historians of late antiquity.

Roger Chartier, *Cultural History between Practices and Representations* (Cambridge, 1988). Eight essays on early modern France designed to illustrate major problems in cultural history.

Alain Corbin, *The Foul and the Fragrant: Odor and the French Social Imagination* (1982; English trans. Leamington Spa, 1986). The study that put smells on the historical map.

Thomas Crow, *Painters and Public Life in Eighteenth-Century Paris* (Princeton, 1985). A political history of painting, drawing on Habermas and the idea of the public sphere.

Carlo Ginzburg, *Myths, Emblems, Clues* (1986; English trans. 1990). A collection of essays including the famous piece on historical evidence as a series of clues.

Carol Gluck, *Japan's Modern Myths: Ideology in the Late Meiji Period* (Princeton, 1985). An exemplary study of the cultural consequences of westernization and modernization.

Serge Gruzinski, *Conquest of Mexico: The Incorporation of Indian Societies into the Western World* (1988; English trans. Cambridge, 1993). A fine study of cultural encounters and the social imagination.

Gábor Klaniczay, *The Uses of Supernatural Power* (Cambridge, 1990). Ten essays on Central European history, ranging from saints to shamans and from beards to laughter.

Steven Shapin, *A Social History of Truth: Civility and Science in Seventeenth-Century England* (Chicago, 1994). A persuasive combination of social and cultural approaches to the history of science.

Jay Winter, *Sites of Memory, Sites of Mourning: The Great War in European Cultural History* (Cambridge, 1995). Shows how the experience of war may be integrated into the history of culture.

Index

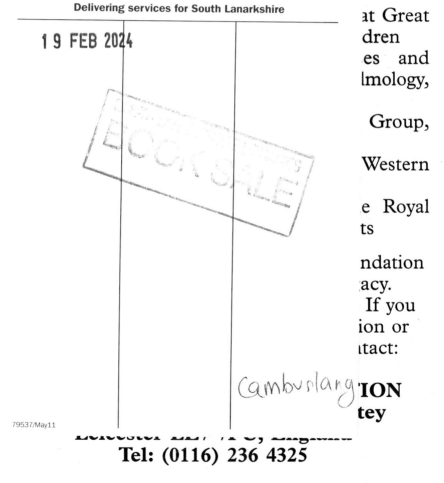

Regarded as a central figure in British modernism whose work was remarked upon by Virginia Woolf as 'the only writing I have ever been jealous of', Katherine Mansfield was born in Wellington, New Zealand in 1888. She travelled to England to study at Queen's College, London, there joining the staff of the *College Magazine*. Back in New Zealand she took up music, becoming an accomplished cellist, but found she could not settle down in Wellington society, and in 1908 left for Europe permanently.

The author of numerous short stories, articles and book reviews for magazines, including the socialist *The New Age* and the literary *Athenaeum*, Mansfield adopted a bohemian lifestyle, enjoying love affairs with both men and women, and finding a place in the circle of intellectual modernists such as D. H. Lawrence and Virginia Woolf. Both her intense grief at the death of her brother Leslie, killed whilst serving in the First World War, and nostalgia for New Zealand, were to have a profound influence upon her later writing.